NATIONAL THEATRE OF SCOTLAND

The National Theatre of Scotland presents

THE WHEEL

by Zinnie Harris

The Wheel was first presented by the National Theatre of Scotland at the Traverse Theatre, Edinburgh, on 7 August 2011. The cast, in alphabetical order, was as follows:

Girl	Rebecca Benson
Blandine / Woman / Thi	Elizabeth Chan
Tomas / Jacques / Teenage Boy	Ryan Fletcher
Madame / Hanna	Meg Fraser
Rossignol	Paul Thomas Hickey
Juan / Pierre / Xuan	Orion Lee
Colline / Glennister	Stephen McCole
Pedro / Farshad	Mark Monero
Beatriz	Catherine Walsh
Rosa	Olga Wehrly
Sargento / Hancock	Leo Wringer
Moreno / Jozka / Clement	Benny Young
Boy	Cameron Gallagher / Zak McCullough
Little Girl	Stephanie Irwin / Lula Molleson

Writer	Zinnie Harris
Director	Vicky Featherstone
Movement Director	Christine Devaney
Set & Costume Designer	Merle Hensel
Composer & Sound Designer	Nick Powell
Lighting Designer	Natasha Chivers
Effects Designer	Jamie Harrison
Assistant Director	Phil McCormack
Casting Director	Anne Henderson

Company Stage Manager	Kate Ferris
Technical Stage Manager	Sam Thornber
Deputy Stage Manager	Fiona Kennedy
Assistant Stage Manager	Katie Hutcheson
Assistant Stage Manager	Niamh O'Meara
Sound Supervisor	Chris Reid
Lighting Supervisor	James Gardner
Wardrobe Supervisor	Ali Currie
Wardrobe Assistant	Janice Burgos
Wardrobe Assistant	Kat Smith

The Cast

Rebecca Benson
Girl

Rebecca recently graduated from the Royal Scottish Academy of Music and Drama.

Work for the National Theatre of Scotland includes *365* and she made her professional stage debut with the Company in *Little Otik*.

Other theatre credits include *What I Meant Was…, Gilgamesh, Richard III, Uncle Vanya, The Glass Menagerie* (RSAMD) and *Top Table* (Òran Mór).

Film work includes *You Instead* and *Blackwaterside*.

Elizabeth Chan
Blandine / Woman caught on barbed wire / Thi

Elizabeth trained at École Philippe Gaulier, Paris, and Drama Centre London.

Theatre work includes *Greenland* (National, London), *Don't Shoot the Clowns* (Fuel), *An Argument about Sex* (Traverse/ Tramway), *Cinderella* (Lyric, Hammersmith), *Bacchaefull* (Dirty Market), *Monkey!* (Polka), *Ya Get Me* (Old Vic), *Nicholas Nickleby, Age Sex Loc@tion, 2.18 Underground,* and *Kissing Angels* (National Youth Theatre).

Television work includes *Coronation Street, Spirit Warriors* and *Silent Witness*.

Ryan Fletcher
Tomas / Jacques / Teenage Boy

Ryan trained at the Royal Scottish Academy of Music and Drama.

Work for the National Theatre of Scotland includes *Beautiful Burnout, Cockroach, Nobody Will Ever Forgive Us, 365* and *The Wolves in the Walls*. Ryan was also a member of the original cast of the multi-award winning *Black Watch* and toured with the production in the UK and internationally from 2006 – 2008.

Other theatre credits include *A Midsummer Night's Dream, Turbo Folk, Cyrano de Bergerac, Water-proof, Ae Fond Kiss, An Advert for the Army, Before I Go* (Òran Mór), *The Costorphine Road Nativity* (Festival Theatre, Edinburgh), *The Last Witch* (EIF/ Traverse) and *Confessions of a Justified Sinner* (Royal Lyceum, Edinburgh).

Film and television credits include *Limmy's Show, Walking Wounded, Stately Suicide, Taggart, Scottish Killers, Filthy Rich,The Night Sweeper* and *Stop, Look, Listen*. Ryan was also a series regular in *River City* for BBC Scotland.

Meg Fraser

Madame / Hanna

Meg trained at the Royal Scottish Academy of Music and Drama.

Her previous work for the National Theatre of Scotland includes *Cockroach*.

Other theatre credits include *Fall, Nova Scotia* (Traverse), *The Night Before Christmas* (Belgrade Theatre, Coventry), *Tom Fool* (Citizens, Glasgow – Critics' Award for Theatre in Scotland, Best Female Performance, 2007), *All My Sons* (Royal Lyceum, Edinburgh – TMA Best Supporting Actress), *Being Norwegian* (Paines Plough/ Òran Mór), *Game Theory* (Ek Productions), *What I Heard About Iraq* (James Seabright/ Paul Lucas Productions), *Eric LaRue* (Royal Shakespeare Company/ Soho), *Twelfth Night, As You Like It, Hamlet, Macbeth* (RSC), *Julius Caesar, The Taming of the Shrew, The Playboy of the Western World* (Royal Lyceum, Edinburgh). For three years, Meg was a member of Dundee Rep Ensemble where her performances included *The Winter's Tale, The Seagull, Mince* and *Cabaret*.

Film and television work includes *Young Adam* and *Taggart*. Radio work includes *The Pillow Book, The Tenderness of Wolves, The Trick is to Keep Breathing* and *Gondwanaland*.

Paul Thomas Hickey

Rossignol

Paul's work for the National Theatre of Scotland includes *Roman Bridge*.

Other theatre credits include *What We Know, The Slab Boys Trilogy, Gagarin Way, Passing Places* (Traverse), *Romeo and Juliet, The Talented Mr Ripley, If Destroyed True* (Dundee Rep), *Strawberries in January, Crave* (Paines Plough), *San Diego, The Tempest* (Tron), *Mainstream, Timeless* (Suspect Culture), *The Backroom* (Bush), *The Slab Boys Trilogy* (Young Vic), *A.D., Ecstasy* (Raindog), *Shining Souls* (Old Vic) and *Once More with Feeling* (Tramway).

Film and television credits include *Believe, Perfect Sense, Hope Springs, The Bill, Taggart, Nightlife, Cardiac Arrest, The Jacobites, Sweetest Feeling* and *Tinseltown*.

Orion Lee

Juan / Pierre / Xuan

Orion trained at the London Academy of Music and Dramatic Arts.

Theatre work includes *Enron* (Headlong), *Passport to Pimlico, On the Boost, The Permanent Way, The Man of Mode, The Maid's Tragedy, The Prisoner's Dilemma, Twelfth Night, The Cherry Orchard* and *Our Boys* (LAMDA).

Film and television work includes *The Jury II, Silent Witness, Creeping Zero* and *Macbeth No More*.

Stephen McCole

Colline / Glennister

Stephen's theatre work includes *Monks* (Royal Lyceum, Edinburgh), *Blood Wedding, Romeo and Juliet* (Citizens, Glasgow), *The Above* (Òran Mór), *Losing Alec* (Cumbernauld) and *Trainspotting* (G&J Productions).

Television work includes *Field of Blood, Single Father, High Times, Taggart, Rebus, Holby City, The Key, Band of Brothers* and *The Young Person's Guide to Being a Rock Star*. Radio includes *Quartet*.

Film credits include a *Lonely Place to Die, Neds, Perfect Sense, Crying with Laughter, Stone of Destiny, Kitchen, The Magdalene Sisters, Last Orders, Complicity, The Acid House, Orphans* and *Rushmore*.

Mark Monero

Pedro / Farshad

Trained at Anna Scher Theatre.

Theatre work includes *Adrenaline Heart* (Bush), *Pure Gold, Christ of Cold Harbour Lane* (Soho), *Measure for Measure* (Almeida), *Pepper Soup* (Lyric Hammermsith), *Invisible* (King's Head), *Sing Yer Heart Out* and *Local Boy* (tour).

Television work includes *Doctor Who, Casualty, The Bill, Skins, Trial and Retribution, Doctors, Waking the Dead, Murphy's Law, Judge John Deed, Silver Street, Gimme, Gimme, Gimme, Young, Gifted and Broke, Lovejoy, Dempsey and Makepeace, The Lenny Henry Show, Grange Hill*, and for many years Mark played the character Steve Elliot in *EastEnders*.

Film work includes *Somers Town, Wilt, A Prayer for the Dying, Babylon, Sid and Nancy* and *Wild Bill*.

Catherine Walsh

Beatriz

Catherine trained at the Samuel Beckett Centre, Trinity College, Dublin.

Her theatre work includes *Dancing At Lughnasa, A Christmas Carol, Phaedra* (Gate, Dublin), *The New Electric Ballroom (Galway Arts Festival/ Edinburgh International Festival/ St Ann's Warehouse, New York), Playboy of the Western World, The Shadow of the Glen* (Druid/ Galway/ EIF/ Lincoln Centre, New York), *Sharon's Grave, Werewolves, The Year of the Hiker* (Druid), *The Empress of India* (Druid/ Abbey, Dublin), *At Swim Two Birds, Fool For Love* (Peacock, Dublin), *Eden, The Passing, Translations, Love in the Title, Kevin's Bed, Blackwater Angel, The Gigli Concert* (Abbey), *From Both Hips* (Tricycle/ Fishamble), *Licking the Marmalade Spoon* (Project), *Buddleia* (Project/ Donmar/ Kontac Festival, Poland) and *Sardines* (Pigsback).

Television work includes *Holby City, Private Lives, Family, The Ambassador* and *On Home Ground*.

Catherine won the Irish Times/ESB Best Actress of the Year in 2001 for her performance in *Eden* at the Abbey Theatre, Dublin.

Olga Wehrly

Rosa

Olga's theatre work includes *Penelope* (Druid, winner of a Fringe First, 2010), *Helter Skelter*, *Red Light Winter* (PurpleHeart), *Macbeth, Othello* (Second Age), *Blind Spot, Drapes (Fishamble Whereabouts)* and *Sexual Perversity in Chicago* (Icarus).

Television work includes *The Galway Races, This is Nightlive, Flirtysomething, Raw, Ape, The Clinic* and *Uri's Haunted Venice*.

Film work includes the features *Death of a Superhero, One Christmas Eve, The Alarms, Speed Dating* and the short films *Blood Coloured Moon, Nuts, Team Sleep* and *The Crush,* which was nominated for an Academy Award in 2011.

Leo Wringer

Sargento / Hancock

Leo went to the Guildhall School of Music and Drama.

His theatre credits include *The Snow Queen* (Royal Lyceum, Edinburgh), *While You Lie* (Traverse), *Julius Caesar, The Taming of the Shrew, Othello* (Shakespeare at the Tobacco Factory, Bristol), *King Lear, Romeo and Juliet, The Comedy of Errors* (Royal Shakespeare Company), *Medea* (Queens), *The Winter's Tale* (Complicite), *Sanctuary* (National, London), *Two Horsemen* (Bush), *Divine Right* (Birmingham Rep) and *Search and Destroy* (Royal Court).

Television work includes *Silent Witness, The Bill, Rebus, Rough Crossings, Murphy's Law, Judge John Deed, Casualty, Canterbury Tales, Love Hurts* and *Escape from Kampala*.

Film work includes *The Changeling* and *The Kitchen Toto*.

Benny Young

Moreno / Jozka / Clement

Benny's previous work for the National Theatre of Scotland includes *Be Near Me* and *Six Characters in Search of an Author*.

Other theatre credits include *Sub Rosa* (Fire Exit), *Staircase* (Tron), *The Importance of Being Alfred* (Òran Mór), *The Grapes of Wrath* (Chichester), *The Tobacco Merchant's Lawyer* (Tron/Traverse), *Six Acts of Love, The Drawer Boy* (Tron), *Night Time* (Traverse), *Hughie* (Arches), *The Crucible, A View from the Bridge, Hobson's Choice* (The Touring Consortium), *The Iceman Cometh* (Old Vic) and seasons with the National Theatre, London, the Royal Shakespeare Company and the Royal Lyceum Theatre, Edinburgh.

Television work includes *Scottish Killers, Garrow's Law, Waking The Dead: Sins of the Father, Spooks, Talk to Me, Taggart, Coronation Street, Boon, Playing the Field, The Kid in the Corner, The Funny Man, The Bill, Between The Lines, Doctor Finlay, Family Affairs* and *Tell Tale Hearts*.

Film work includes *Chariots of Fire, Out of Africa* and *White Nights*.

Creative Team

Zinnie Harris

Writer

Zinnie is a playwright, screenwriter and theatre director.

For the National Theatre of Scotland she adapted and directed *Julie,* a new version of August Strindberg's *Miss Julie,* which toured Scotland in 2006.

Her other plays include *The Panel, A Doll's House, The Garden, Fall, Solstice, Midwinter, Nightingale and Chase, Further than the Furthest Thing* and *By Many Wounds.*

Directing work includes *While You Lie, The Garden* (Traverse), *Solstice, Midwinter* (Royal Shakespeare Company) and *Dealer's Choice* (Tron).

Awards include the Arts Foundation Award for Playwriting (2004), and for *Further than the Furthest Thing,* the Peggy Ramsay Foundation Award (1999), a Fringe First and a John Whiting Award (2000).

Television credits include *Born with Two Mothers, Richard is my Boyfriend* and *Spooks.*

She is currently an Associate Artist at the Traverse Theatre, Edinburgh.

Vicky Featherstone

Director

Vicky is the Artistic Director of the National Theatre of Scotland.

Her directing work for the National Theatre of Scotland includes *Wall of Death: A Way of Life* (co-directed with Stephen Skrynka), *Long Gone Lonesome, The Miracle Man, Empty, Cockroach, 365, Mary Stuart* and *The Wolves in the Walls* (co-directed with Julian Crouch, TMA Award for Best Children's Show, 2006). Forthcoming directing projects include Abi Morgan's *27.*

Previously, Vicky was Artistic Director of new writing theatre company Paines Plough. Her awards include six Fringe Firsts, TMA Best Director and two Herald Angels.

Vicky has also worked in television as a drama executive for the BBC, Granada TV and Central TV. She created several original drama series, including *Where the Heart Is* and *Silent Witness.* Vicky is a trustee of the Royal Scottish Academy of Music and Drama and Glasgow Science Centre.

Christine Devaney

Movement Director

Christine trained at London Contemporary Dance School. She was a founding member of Dundee Rep Dance Company (currently Scottish Dance Theatre) and for nine years performed and was associate director with V-tol Dance Company.

Work for the National Theatre of Scotland includes *Venus as a Boy*, as co-director, and *Something Wicked This Way Comes*, as choreographer.

Recent work includes directing *Spokes* (All Or Nothing/ Strange Bird Zircus), and the choreography for *Around the World in 80 Days* (Lung Ha).

Other companies Christine has worked with include Frantic Assembly, The Kosh, Quarantine, Plan B, Yolander Snaith Theatre Dance, TAG, The Unicorn, Leicester Haymarket and Catherine wheels Theatre Company.

Christine is Artistic Director of Edinburgh-based Curious Seed and is an associate artist with Imaginate.

Merle Hensel

Set & Costume Designer

Merle trained as a theatre designer at Central St Martin's School of Art and Design and the Slade School of Fine Art, London.

Theatre credits include *Shun-Kin* (Complicite/ Setagaya/ Barbican), *James Son of James, The Bull, The Flowerbed* (Fabulous Beast/ Barbican/ Dublin Theatre Festival), *Political Mother* (Hofesh Schechter Company/ Sadler's Wells), *Justita, Park* (Jasmin Vardimon Dance Company/ Peacock, London), *Parallel Elektra* (Young Vic), *The Girls of Slender Means* (Stellar Quines), *Cat on a Hot Tin Roof* (Corn Exchange/ Dublin Theatre Festival), *Der Diener Zweier Herren* (Max-Reinhardt Seminar/ Schlosstheater, Vienna); *Before the Wolf* (Open Air Festivals Newcastle and Falkirk), *Human Shadows* (Underground/ The Place Prize, London); *Ippolit* (Sophiensaele, Berlin/ Schauspielhaus, Zürich/ Münchner Kammerspiele), *Der Verlorene* (Sophiensaele, Berlin), *Kupsch* (Deutsches Theater, Göttingen), *Maria Stuarda* (Vereinigte Bühnen, Mönchengladbach/ Krefeld), *Der Vetter aus Dingsda* (Oper Graz), *Münchhausen* and *Herr der Lügen* (Neuköllner Oper, Berlin).

Film credits include *Morituri te salutant* and *Baby*.

Merle is a lecturer at Central St Martin's School of Art and Design. Other teaching includes Rose Bruford College and Goldsmiths, London.

Nick Powell

Composer & Sound Designer

Nick's work for the National Theatre of Scotland includes *Dunsinane, Realism, The Wonderful World of Dissocia, Futurology: A Global Review* and *The Wolves in the Walls*.

Other recent work for theatre includes *Get Santa, The Priory, Relocated, The Vertical Hour* (Royal Court), *The Lord of the Flies, The Crucible* (Open Air Theatre, Regent's Park), *The Drunks, The Grainstore* (Royal Shakespeare Company), *Falstaff* (Centro Dramático Nacional, Madrid), *Penumbra, Tito Andronico* (Animalario, Madrid), *Urtain, Marat-Sade* (Animalario/ CDN, Spain), *Paradise* (Ruhr Triennale Festival), *Panic* (Improbable/ Barbican/ Sydney Opera House) and *The Family Reunion* (Donmar).

Television work includes *Beneath the Veil, Death in Gaza, Lip Service* and the Spanish feature *Dispongo de Barcos*. He has also scored three of the films of visual artist Phil Collins.

Nick has toured and recorded with many bands including McAlmont & Butler, Strangelove, and Astrid. He is one half of OSKAR, who have performed live scores for three Prada fashion shows in Milan, exhibited installations at the V&A, London and the CCA, Glasgow.

Awards include the Spanish 2010 Max for Best Composition in Scenic Arts.

Natasha Chivers

Lighting Designer

Natasha's work for the National Theatre of Scotland includes *The House of Bernarda Alba, The Miracle Man, Empty, Mary Stuart, The Wolves in the Walls* and *HOME Glasgow*.

Other theatre work includes *The Horse You Rode In On* (Told By An Idiot), *Happy Days* (Sheffield Crucible), *Statement of Regret* (National, London), *That Face* (Royal Court/Duke of York), *Renaissance, Run!* (Greenwich and Docklands International Festival), *Beyond Belief* (Carriageworks, Sydney), *Dirty Wonderland* (Frantic Assembly/ Brighton Festival), *Love* (VesturPort) plus work for many other companies including Frantic Assembly and Lyric Hammersmith.

Dance work includes *Electric Hotel* (Fuel/ Sadler's Wells), *Scattered* (Motionhouse) and *Electric Counterpoint* (Royal Opera House).

Natasha won the 2007 Olivier Award for Best Lighting Design for *Sunday in the Park with George*.

Jamie Harrison

Effects Designer

Jamie trained at the Royal Academy of Music and Drama.

He recently worked with the National Theatre of Scotland on *Peter Pan*.

Jamie is Artistic Director of Vox Motus. With Candice Edmunds, Jamie has written, directed and designed all Vox Motus's work to date, including *Slick, Bright Black* and *The Not So Fatal Death of Grandpa Fredo*.

As a magician, Jamie has worked in 22 countries across Europe, Asia and the US for clients including Motorola, Sony and Pricewaterhouse Coopers. He regularly works as an illusion and effect designer for theatres and companies across the UK.

Jamie is currently a creative consultant for the Olympic Festival on Exhibition Road during London 2012.

Phil McCormack

Assistant Director

Phil trained at the Royal Scottish Academy of Music and Drama.

Phil recently completed a year as Trainee Associate with the National Theatre of Scotland. Assistant Directing credits with the Company include *Transform Glasgow: Smiler, Extreme* and *Nothing to See Here*. He was Associate Artist on *Transform East Renfrewshire: One-All*. Later this year, he will be Assistant Director on *Men Should Weep*.

Devising and directing credits include *Palimpsest** (Situate Performance), *This is a Photograph of Her* (a performance residency at HMP Corton Vale), *The Only Things Certain in Life* (RSAMD). Other work while training includes *Unit, Awkward Spaces* and *Public Displays of Rhythm*.

Placement supported by the Federation of Scottish Theatre, with funding from Creative Scotland.

About the National Theatre of Scotland

In 2011, the National Theatre of Scotland celebrates its first five years of creating theatre that excites and entertains audiences at home and beyond, and which makes Scotland proud.

Since our very first productions in 2006, everything we have aspired to challenges the notion of what theatre can achieve. With no building of our own we're free to make theatre wherever we can connect with an audience – a promise we take seriously. Our work has been shown in airports and high-rises, forests and ferries, drill halls and football pitches, pubs and factories.

As Scotland's national theatre, we exist to work collaboratively with the best companies and individuals to produce and tour world class theatre that's for the people, led by great performances, great writers and great stories.

National Theatre of Scotland
Civic House,
26 Civic Street,
Glasgow G4 9RH

T: +44 (0) 141 221 0970
F: +44 (0) 141 331 0589
E: info@nationaltheatrescotland.com

www.nationaltheatrescotland.com

The Scottish
Government

The National Theatre of Scotland is core funded by the Scottish Government.

The National Theatre of Scotland, a company limited by guarantee and registered in Scotland (SC234270), is a registered Scottish charity (SC033377).

Zinnie Harris
The Wheel

ff

faber and faber

First published in 2011
by Faber and Faber Limited
74–77 Great Russell Street, London WC1B 3DA

Typeset by Country Setting, Kingsdown, Kent CT14 8ES
Printed in England by CPI Bookmarque, Croydon, Surrey

A CIP record for this book
is available from the British Library

ISBN 978-0-571-28215-9

2 4 6 8 10 9 7 5 3 1

For my Dad

*with love, admiration and a jar
full of butterflies . . .*

Acknowledgements

I want to thank the following people for their help and support as I shaped and formed *The Wheel*: Frances Poet, Mel Kenyon, John Harris, David Harrower, Dominic Hill, Gemma Chan, Eileen Walsh, Benny Young, Orion Lee, Munir Khairdin, Andy Clark, David Hayman, Taqi Nazeer, Kate Dickie, Molly Innes, Brian Ferguson, Gerry Mulgrew, Ian Dunn, Keith Fleming, Finn Den Hertog, Paul Chan, Gail Watson and Rebecca Benson. Above all I want to thank Vicky Featherstone for her belief, encouragement and careful attention to detail that has sustained me on the journey. Three years ago, standing in the Traverse foyer, Vicky lent me a pen. As I took it she added, with typical quick-wittedness, that I would have to write a play for her in return. Vicky, thanks for the pen. Here's the play . . .

Characters

Beatriz
a woman from Northern Spain

Rosa
her sister

Pedro
a local farmhand

Juan
a second farmhand

Tomas
Rosa's betrothed

Sargento
the sergeant

Colline
the accused

Moreno
the deputy

A Girl

Rossignol
a naturalist

Blandine
a woman on fire

A Boy

Madame
a doctor's wife

A Woman
caught on barbed wire

A Baby

Jacques
a French soldier

Pierre
his friend

Hanna
a woman from Metz

Hanna's Teenage Son

Jozka
a train conductor for the Trans-European Express

Thi
a Vietnamese woman

Hancock
an American marine

Glennister
Hancock's superior officer

Xuan
Thi's husband

Farshad
a man in the desert

Clement
an old man

THE WHEEL

ONE
PITCHFORKS

A peaceful village in Northern Spain.
The year is late in the nineteenth century; skirts are worn long.
In front of a small house is a large courtyard.
In the middle of the courtyard is a large table.
Overhead are vines.
A woman, Beatriz, brings on a piece of cloth and a basin of water.
She takes the cloth and scrubs the table.
Beatriz is beautiful, but this is a hot day and it's hard work.
She squeezes the cloth and scrubs again.
When she is satisfied, she takes a large white sheet and puts it over the table.
She spreads down the corners.
She tucks the sides under.
The sheet is stained and has a hole.
She tries to move the sheet, so the hole is less visible.
It doesn't really work.
The sheet is tatty by anyone's standards.
Beatriz goes into the house and gets a jug of water. She puts it over the hole.
She hangs some garlands in the vines.
A second woman, Rosa, comes in.
Rosa is younger than Beatriz by a few years and is wearing a petticoat.
She sits down in a chair.

Beatriz
    You're not ready?

Rosa

It's so hot.
We should be sleeping. We should be flat on our backs in the shade.

Beatriz

Two hours, that's all.

Rosa

I know.
Pass me the cloth.

Beatriz

It's dirty, I just cleaned the table.

Rosa

The water then.

Beatriz passes her the jug.
Rosa takes some water and puts it behind her neck.
Cools herself down.

You want some?

Beatriz

No.

Beatriz carries on laying the table.
Rosa pours the water down her breasts and shoulders.

Rosa

I used the lemon juice like you said.

She lifts her petticoat to look at her legs.

Don't think it did any good. Still black as anything.
Look.
Still the worst kind of spider crawling up my legs.

Beatriz

All women have hair.

Rosa

Of course, a little hair is beautiful. Women are

supposed to have a little hair, but like mine? And
my arms are the same. He thinks I am lovely, that's
because the face and the neck and the head, fine,
but the body – when the clothes are off . . . ?

Beatriz

He won't notice.

Rosa

Maybe not the first time, tonight.
Tonight he'll be so keen he'd go with any hairy
animal, but tomorrow? And the day after?

Beatriz

He's seen you before.

Rosa

It was dark.

Beatriz

So stay in the dark.

Rosa

Our whole lives?
Anyway I have veins.

Beatriz

For goodness sake.

Rosa

I know, sorry. Shut up shut up.
I didn't sleep last night.

Beatriz

Worrying about your veins?

Rosa

Partly.

Beatriz smiles.

Don't laugh.

Beatriz laughs.

Stop it. It's serious.

Beatriz
Deadly.

Rosa laughs a little too. Despite herself.

Rosa
I wish you could make love with your clothes on.

Beatriz
You can.

Rosa
Some of them.

Beatriz
He's probably thinking exactly the same thing. He's
probably standing looking in the mirror at his father's
house agonising about his bent whatsit, and the boil
on his behind.

Rosa laughs.

You're made for each other.

Rosa
Do you think?

Beatriz
Absolutely.
Tomas and Rosa, written in the vines.
And the sooner the sun moves across the sky, and the
priest rings the bell and we get on with this the better.

*Beatriz gets some baskets of bread and puts them on the
table.*

Rosa
I don't know how you can move around, aren't you hot?

Beatriz
You should get dressed.

Rosa
Not yet.
I like this. With you.
This has to be the hottest day this year, don't you think?

Beatriz
Maybe.

Rosa
It was really hot in the night.

Beatriz
Tonight will be hotter.

Rosa
Stop it.

Beatriz
It was just an observation. About the weather.

Rosa
You're teasing me.

Beatriz continues to put cups on the table.

Madame Creole said she'd give us two chickens, did I tell you?

Beatriz
No.

Rosa
And Jan a wooden chair.

Beatriz
A wooden chair?

Rosa
Yes.

Beatriz
Oh.

Rosa
Well, one is better than none.

Beatriz
I suppose.

Rosa
We've got no table to put it under anyway.
There's pink in the milk.

Beatriz looks.

Beatriz
I think the jug was dirty.

Rosa
I noticed it yesterday as well.
If the goat's not well –

Beatriz
The goat's fine.

Rosa
Would you tell me?
If the goat were to die –

Beatriz
I'd survive.

Rosa
You'd have nothing.

Beatriz
Then I'd come knocking at your door.

*Beatriz takes a pewter object and puts it back on the
table.*

Rosa
What's that?

Beatriz
I found it in the cupboard, I think you are meant to put candles in it –

Rosa
It's horrible.

Beatriz
It used to be Papa's.

Rosa
Does that mean we have to use it?

Beatriz
No, but I thought it might be nice.

Rosa
Nice?

Beatriz
With candles.

Rosa
We've got the sun, why do we need candles?

Beatriz
OK, it's your wedding.
I just thought –

Beatriz looks at it.
It's true, it's horrible.

Pity, I was going to give it to you.

Rosa
Give it to me . . . ?

Beatriz
I don't have anything else.

Rosa
You've given me all this.

Beatriz

It's not so bad.

Rosa

Beatriz –

Beatriz

The poor man's gone, the least we could do is light
his candles.
He can't walk you down the aisle,
He can't even see you like this today.

Rosa

He probably hated it.
He probably only kept it because it was his father's.
And his father's before him.
The misery of this candlestick has probably gone on
for generations.

Beatriz

I think if you put a few ribbons around it –

Rosa

No.
Beatriz, no.
Not even for him.

Beatriz takes it off the table.

What if I were to tell you there were three jugs of
wine behind the wheel?

Beatriz

Wine?

Rosa

What would you say? Better than a candlestick.

Beatriz

I'd say you're mad.

Rosa

Or magic.

Beatriz
Where did you get it?

Rosa
That's the question.

Beatriz
There isn't any wine, the grapes failed.

Rosa
Out of thin air then.

Beatriz
You stole it?

Rosa
Not quite.

Beatriz
Madam Creole –

Rosa
Has more than enough.

Beatriz
And if she finds out?

Rosa
How would she find out? I've carried it here egg cup
by egg cup.
I hid it under my skirt, or in my hat.
I had to go the long way round so I missed the bridge,
careful not to spill a drop. Three years ago it was us
that had the wine, and she that was begging.

Beatriz
Rosa –?

Rosa
It's a wedding. Don't be cross.

Beatriz
I'm not cross, I'm worried.

Rosa

Don't be worried.

She produces some wine.

Want a taste then?

Beatriz

Three jugs . . . ?

Rosa

You are cross.

Beatriz

Do you know how much this would fetch?

Rosa

I'm sure you're going to tell me.

Beatriz

More than both of us live off in a year, two maybe.

Rosa

Tastes good though. We'll get blinding drunk, we'll
end up with a headache, and Tomas will drink so
much it will be the middle of next week before he
realises he's married a baboon.

Beatriz laughs.
*Rosa puts her finger in. She holds it out for Beatriz to
taste.*
Beatriz tastes.
So does Rosa.

Good?

Beatriz

Don't spill it.

Rosa

I won't spill it.

She puts the three jugs on the table.

Beatriz

Put a plate over them then. So no flies get in.

They put plates over the wine.
Beatriz smiles.

Anyway, as far as baboons go, you're beautiful,
One of the best.
Now do your hair.
The ones on your head.

Beatriz goes inside.
Rosa picks up a hairbrush.
She starts to do her hair.
She takes out a mirror.
She looks at herself.
The face is OK.
She smiles.
She lifts the skirt, looks at the legs in the mirror.
Ugh. The legs are still hairy.
Puts the skirt back down.
Undoes her blouse a little. Looks at the top of her breasts.
She lifts them up, sees if she can improve her cleavage.
A man comes in and watches.

Pedro

Nice, I would say.

Rosa turns away, does up her blouse.

You were looking for an opinion.

Rosa

Get out of here.

Pedro

The gate was open.

Rosa

Who are you?

Pedro

A man. A randy man if you open your blouse again.

Rosa stands up, moves away.

Don't look like that. I've been walking for twelve hours. I saw the house. I thought you might have some water.

Rosa

Nothing.

Pedro

Not even a small drop?
I'm as thirsty as all hell.

Rosa

Then you'll leave?

Pedro

Yes.

Rosa

Straight away, and shut the gate behind you?

Pedro

Of course.

Rosa gets him a cup and goes to the tap.

What's in the jug?

Rosa

Nothing.
Don't touch.

Pedro

Why not?

He lifts the lid.

Wow.

Rosa

We're having a wedding.

Pedro

Where the hell did you get it?

Rosa

You asked for some water.

Pedro

Before I knew what else you had.
You must have miracle soil.

Rosa

We're careful with our wine.

Pedro

You must be.

He sits down.

Rosa

You touch it, it's theft.

Pedro

A second theft?

He drinks the water.

Where's the bride?

Rosa

She isn't here.

Pedro

What a pity.
Brides are good luck.

Rosa

It'll be small, hardly anyone –

Pedro

Quite a spread for hardly anyone.

Rosa

I think you should drink your water and go.

Pedro

Problem is, my mouth's salivating. I haven't had wine since year before last.

He holds up his cup.

I'll toast the bride's good fortune.
You say no, I'll say a curse.

Rosa

I don't believe in curses.

Pedro

Lucky you aren't the bride then.

Beat.
Pedro isn't going anywhere.

Rosa

One small glass?

Pedro

Then I'll go.

Rosa goes to the jug. She pours him one small glass of wine.

Can I see your tits again?

Rosa

Get lost.

Pedro drinks the wine.
Rosa puts the plate back on the jug, and moves it away.
Pedro has finished, he puts the glass back down on the table.
He yells.

Pedro

Oi. Over here.

Rosa

What are you doing?

Pedro
    He's my friend.

Rosa
    You said you'd go.

Pedro
    Never trust a soldier.

Rosa
    You're not a soldier, you're a farmhand.

Pedro
    We're all soldiers now.
    Haven't you heard?

Rosa
    No?

Pedro
    France has marched in. Come right over the hill.

A second man walks in, Juan.

Rosa
    When?

Juan
    Is that cake I can smell?

Rosa
    Tell him to turn around, go back.

Pedro
    Why would I do that?

Rosa
    We've got a wedding in an hour.

Juan
    We'll be very good. You'll hardly notice us.

The second man sits down.

Rosa
> You can't do this.

Juan
> You've got oranges . . .?

Pedro
> And wine.

Juan
> Wine?

Rosa
> Don't touch it.

Rosa comes and takes away the second jug of wine.

> When did France march in?

Juan
> Give us the wine and we'll tell you everything.

Rosa
> Bugger off.

Rosa moves away.
Pedro grabs her.
She holds on to it,
And the wine spills on the cloth.

> You bloody idiot.

Pedro
> You idiot.
> We could have drunk that.

Rosa
> We could have drunk that. Get off.

A tussle.

> I'd rather throw it into the ground, than let you have it.

Pedro
> Is that so?

Beatriz comes back in.

Beatriz
Oi, thieves.

Juan
We aren't thieves, we're guests.

Rosa
Guests that weren't invited.

Pedro
Not true.

Rosa
Liar.

Pedro
Tomas told us where to come.

Rosa
Tomas wouldn't even talk to rats like you.

Pedro
He even showed us the way.
Told us there'd be food, some water.

Rosa
He wouldn't do that.

Beatriz
Get off, you vermin.

Juan
Ask him yourself.

Rosa
I will when he gets here.

Juan
Lucky for you, he's just coming.

Rosa
Tomas . . . ?

Tomas walks in. He is not dressed for a wedding.

Tomas

People are being killed, Rosa. Listen to me.

Rosa

You brought them here?

Tomas

They've been marching, they were thirsty.

Rosa

This is our wedding day.

Tomas

We can't get married with this going on.
Did you hear about France?

Rosa

I heard.

Tomas

So we need to be strong for the fight –

Rosa

For the fight?

Tomas

OK, listen to me. I don't want this, none of us do. But
what do you expect, we do nothing? And then what –
tomorrow we wake up French? See a fucking French
palace built in San Sebastian. Is that what you want?

Rosa

Of course not.

Tomas

You should be proud of me.

Rosa

You expect too much.

She pulls the tablecloth. Everything falls on the floor.

Go on then, eat it off the floor
You ants.

Tomas
Rosa!

*The other men have salvaged some food from the ground.
Another man walks in, the Sergeant.*

Sargento
How many beds? Can we sleep here?

Juan
The house looks well equipped.

Pedro
Stable behind.

Beatriz
What?

Tomas
I didn't say they could all come.

Juan
And a goat I saw.

Tomas
We don't need a goat, surely?

Sargento
Do an inventory. Good women, you're serving Spain
now.
And you'll be rewarded.

Beatriz
Rewarded?

Sargento
You'll be paid for everything that we use.

Beatriz
In what exactly?

Sargento

You write a chitty, I take it to the General.

Beatriz

And what does he do with it?
Wipe his arse?

Sargento

Very good.

Beatriz

Don't patronise me, this is trespass.

Sargento

In times of crisis, there is no such thing as trespass.
This is Spain, we pull together.

Beatriz

Don't call this Spain.
This isn't a Spain I recognise.

Sargento

Get the goat, see what shape it's in –

Tomas

Sir, I think we should leave them the goat.

Sargento

You brought us to this place. It's been noted. Looks like room for twenty in the house, the rest can sleep in tents in the field.

Tomas

Twenty?

Sargento

Clear this table, but leave a chair.

Tomas

Please leave them something.

Sargento

What are these things hanging from the trees?

Pedro
   Garlands.

Tomas
   We can't take everything.

Sargento
   Take them down.

Tomas
   They're friends of mine.

Beatriz
   We're no friends of yours.

Tomas
   I'm trying to help you.

Beatriz
   Don't bother.

Tomas
   Rosa?

Sargento
   What's your name?

Beatriz
   Kill the goat.
   You might as well, you're taking everything else.

Sargento
   That's your name? Kill the goat.

Beatriz
   You don't need my name.

Sargento
   I'm interested.

Beatriz
   Pope Benedict V.

The Sergeant laughs.

Sargento

So you're a comedienne?

Beatriz

And you a jokester?

Sargento

What's this, more wit?

Beatriz

This is all wit, surely. You? You're making me laugh.
First you're marching the wrong way, you want to
meet the French, you'd be better going that way.
Second there might've been food here, but he's brought
you into marshland. You'll sink in your sleep. There's
an underground stream, the whole field floods.

Sargento

Is she right?

Tomas

I didn't know that, sir.

Beatriz

He's more stupid than he looks.
You should go back up the track and sleep on the hill.

Sargento

A proper Sergeant.

Beatriz

And your men, you shouldn't be letting them feast
today like this and then talk of rest. You should be
marching them along the lane. Look at them, no
strength, no muscle, you think the French are going
to roll over?

Sargento

What do you know about soldiers?

Beatriz

My father died on the battlefield.
Last time farmhands were required to fight.

The Sergeant looks at his men.
They look ridiculous, a motley crew.

Sargento

Tell me what to do with them, and you've saved your goat.

Beatriz

They're flabby but they aren't stupid.
You can teach them like horses.

Sargento

They say they've an appetite for battle –

Beatriz

This is an appetite for battle?
Sitting around, eating my cheese?

Beat.

They need to see what they are fighting for. They've only heard rumours, take them to where they can see the destruction the French have left. When they see the women wailing give them weapons they know how to use.

Sargento

There's the problem.

Beatriz

The second barn along is full of tools, spades and pitchforks.
When the blood is up, you can do a lot of damage with a pitchfork.

Sargento

Which barn?

Beatriz

I want my house.
You can use the field, the well, the food, but not the house.

Sargento

You're pretty tough.

Beatriz

You told me you were fighting for Spain.
I don't want to wake up French.

The Sergeant nods. Beatriz has got her bargain.

The last barn. By the sign to St Maria.
Under the trough where the cows drink.

Sargento

And him?
Your friend? What should I do with him?

Beatriz

It's up to Rosa, she was to be his bride.
But the milk's been too long in the sun.
There are lumps of yogurt floating.

Beatriz passes her the milk.
Rosa walks towards Tomas.

Tomas

Rosa.

She pours the off milk over Tomas's head.
The other men laugh.
Rosa rubs the bits of yogurt in his hair.

Rosa

I don't know what I ever saw in you.

Tomas

I love you.

Beatriz

That's the biggest joke of all.

There is some commotion offstage, we hear two voices.

Sargento
For heaven's sake –

Pedro
Looks like Colline, sir.

Sargento
Making that noise?

Pedro
He's with Moreno.

Sargento
More trouble, then.

Moreno comes in with Colline, held roughly by the arm.

Moreno
Sergeant, this man is a traitor –

Sargento
A traitor now?

Colline
It's lies –

Moreno
If you'll just hear me out –

Sargento
Treachery is a big accusation.

Colline
You know I love Spain.

Sargento
QUIET. I can't hear either of you when you are screaming.
This is an army, not a brawl of women.

Beat.

Moreno, you start.

Colline

Is this a court, do I need a lawyer?

Sargento

This is a soldiers' hearing.

Moreno

Benetto and Roman. They'll tell you, they saw it all.
Last night, while everyone else was sleeping –

Sargento

Where?

Moreno

Up by the mill. In the trees –

Colline

I wasn't there even, I –

Moreno

They saw you, that birthmark shines in the dark.

Colline

I'm no traitor.

Moreno

He talked to the French.

Sargento

When exactly?

Moreno

Midnight. Through the night.

Colline

I spoke to them I admit, but not three words.

Sargento

What words?

Colline

I trade with those men.
Yesterday they sold me something, I sold them
something.

Pedro

That I can back up, we've all traded with –

Sargento

WILL YOU HOLD YOUR TONGUE?

He walks close to Colline.

You may have traded with them in the past, but now –

Colline

They owed me money, they're farmers just like us.

Moreno

They're the enemy.

Colline

I have fourteen acres, a debt is a debt.

Sargento

You took money?

Moreno

It's a bribe.

Colline

Sir, believe what you want, but I love my country.
Why would I take a bribe?

Moreno

To lead us into the line of attack.

Colline

And get my friends killed?

Moreno

His father was French.

Colline

In name only.

Sargento

How much money?

Colline

It was a lot of grain.

Moreno

From where, there is no harvest?

Colline

The debt goes back.

Sargento

Or you thought to profit with information.

Colline

I'm not a traitor, I told you.

Sargento

But all of you are acting for yourselves. Don't think
that I don't know the real reason you have all signed
up. There's nothing to be made from the fields this
year, the wage I will pay you is bigger than any other.

Tomas

That's not fair.

Sargento

SILENCE!

Beat.

Where is the money?

Moreno

Here.

He passes the Sergeant a purse.
The Sergeant takes it.
There is a lot of money.

Sargento

It's not insignificant. This amount.
We do things differently in the army.

Colline

I understand.

Sargento

I have to send a message.
The enemy is the enemy.

Colline

OK, I'll learn from my mistakes, I agree it was stupid.

Sargento

Pass me my knife.

Colline

What, you can't –

Sargento

Moreno, you hold him. Someone else to his other side.

Colline

No.

Pedro

If you kill him you'll have to kill me.

Tomas

And me.

Sargento

Stand in line.

Rosa

Tomas, no.

Beatriz

Cover your eyes, Rosa.

Pedro

We all joined up in trust.

Sargento

YOU'RE PEASANTS!
You had fuck-all else to do.

Rosa
Do something.

Beatriz
I don't know what to do.

Sargento
Get the knife.

Colline looks desperate.

Beatriz
And if word gets out you have no mercy, you're a vicious leader?

Sargento
Shut the woman up.

Beatriz
I believe him, as it happens.
Just so as you know before you put the knife in.

Sargento
You can see into a man's soul now as well, can you?

Beatriz
No, but I can spot a despot and it's the other one.

Sargento
You've gone too far, I liked you before.

Beatriz
His hand twists as he talks
And he stands to gain from this man's downfall.

Sargento
He's my trusted deputy.

Beatriz
His family's land backs on to his. We all know the geography, this is an old farming dispute wrapped up in a new package.

Moreno
Who is this woman?
Can't we rip her up?

Sargento
Yes we can.

Moreno
Then why don't we?

Beat.
Moreno's hand flutters.
The Sergeant stands up, he goes towards Moreno.
He looks into his eyes.

For goodness sake.

Sargento
Does your family's land back on to his?

Moreno
It's irrelevant.

Sargento
Do you stand to gain?

Moreno
Hardly at all.

Moreno's hand flutters.

I have a tic, my hand does that sometimes, you know
that. If I had money for a doctor –

Beat.

Sargento
Colline, come here.

He goes back to Colline.
He puts his knife away.

I don't know what to make of this.
Two men, both of whom I would have trusted –

Beat.

LOOK AT ME.

Colline looks at him.
The Sergeant can't see the answers in his face.
He makes a decision.

Alright. Let him go.

They let him go.

Colline
Thank you.

Sargento
Don't thank me, thank Pope Benedict V here.
But stand up, for God's sake, you'd better get moving.

Colline
What do you mean?

Sargento
You might be free but you'll still be condemned in the
eyes of the men. You'll never lose the accusation.

Colline
What?

Sargento
Three hours, that's all I will give you to get as far
away from here as possible. After that if I or any
soldier from this army see you –

Colline
Leave Spain?

Sargento
Yes, and as fast as you can.

Colline
But my farm is here, my family.

Sargento
Not any more.

Colline looks around at them.

Colline
I can't leave, everything I have –
(*To the other men.*) This isn't fair, we all traded with those guys.

Moreno
Shall I boot him out, sir?
See him on his way?

Colline looks dazed.

Colline
You can't do this. I love my country.

Sargento
You've just lost an hour.
Speak again, and you'll lose two.

Colline
You coward.
The woman was right, this is no longer Spain.

He runs.

Sargento
So, your holiness, justice?

Beatriz shrugs.

Beatriz
Maybe of some kind.

Sargento
Watch him until he's over the hill, Tomas, I want to hear when he's out of sight.

Tomas leaves.

Pedro

He'll be ripped limb from limb if the men catch him.
You know what they're like with deserters.

Sargento

Let's hope he runs fast then.

He turns to Moreno.

If this is an old farming dispute as she says, then so
help you.

Moreno

You can't send me away.

Sargento

No, you're too resourceful.

Moreno

These past days I've been your right-hand man.

Sargento

But I can put you at the front, stripped of all honours,
privileges, out with the rabble.

Moreno

You said yourself I'm too old for fighting.

Sargento

I've changed my mind.

Moreno

My old knees, I can't.

Sargento

Just like an old woman, complaining.
Why can't you fight? You've got fingernails. haven't you?
You've got teeth.

Moreno looks around.

Moreno

Is no one going to speak up for me?
This isn't fair. I'll be ripped to pieces.

The Sergeant turns round to Beatriz to see her reaction.

Sargento
No?
Is this fair?

Beatriz
Fair, but not pretty.

Sargento
Why do you say that?

Beatriz
A grown man almost in tears.

Sargento
Send him away for goodness sake.
Put him in a skirt.

Moreno is taken off.
Tomas brings on a Girl.

Tomas
Sir, she was crying a little way back.

Sargento
So?

Tomas
Clawing at the gate.

Sargento
You're bothering me about a child now?

Tomas
She's Colline's daughter.
The man you just sent away.

Sargento
I dealt with her father, someone else can deal with her.

Beat.

Tomas
But what shall I do with her, sir?

Sargento
Send her back to her mother.

Pedro
Her mother is dead.

Sargento
Why are you looking at me? I know nothing about children.

Juan
She's a bastard anyway, she isn't his wife's.

Beatriz
Well, don't stand her next to me.

Beat.

No way. This is your mistake.

Sargento
You're a woman, aren't you?

Beatriz
So?

The Girl starts to cry.

Juan
How old is it?

Beatriz
She.

Sargento
I've no idea.

Beatriz
Don't look at us, we don't want it.

Tomas

The men will tear it apart. Word will get out about the treachery of the father –

Juan

So we take it down to the forest then?
Lose it.

Sargento

Agreed.

Pedro

Quick flick of the knife.

The Girl cries again.

Beatriz

You're joking, surely?
Tomas?

Juan

We just agreed.

Beatriz

Are you out of your mind? An innocent child?

Sargento

Give me a better solution.

Beatriz

Take her to her father.
Get a horse.
Her father is only a minute ahead. They can leave together.

Juan

The men are tired already, sir.

Beatriz

A child doesn't die because people do nothing, not in Spain.

Sargento
But this is a new Spain, as you already said, it's unrecognisable.

Beatriz
Give me a horse then.
I'll do it.

Juan
We don't have many horses to spare, sir.

Beatriz
Find one.

Pedro
They're resting.

Juan
We'll need them fresh for tomorrow.

Sargento
There's a wheelbarrow by the well.

Beatriz looks.
The men laugh.
She takes the wheelbarrow. The wheel falls off.

Beatriz
Why are you laughing? This isn't funny.

Sargento
It's late, we're all tired.
You've spoken up, now do what you want with it.
We're going to bed.

He walks out.

Beatriz
She's tiny, for God's sake.
He's just there, a minute away.

Juan and Pedro walk past her.

Have none of you any heart?
I can't keep her.
We can't feed ourselves, let alone –
She needs to get to her father.
Oi, don't just walk away from me.
I'll curse you, I'll put a hex on all your houses.

They pay no attention, all walk away.
Tomas is left.

Tomas

I'm with the army now, I have to do as they do.

Beatriz

Of course you do.

Tomas goes too.
Beatriz is left with the Girl.

Are you ready to run, sweetheart?

She comes over and takes her hand.
Rosa has stayed.

Rosa

Don't leave me.

Beatriz

Stay here, don't let them near the house.

Rosa

Beatriz –

Beatriz

He's just there, he can't have got far.

Rosa

And me?

Beatriz

You'll be fine, stay close to Tomas.
I'll be back.

Rosa

It's stupid.
You could be attacked if there are soldiers out there,
then –

Beatriz

So pray that I'm not.

She comes back. She kisses Rosa.

I'll be really quick.

Rosa

Run.

She runs.

TWO
SMOKE

Further on the track.
Beatriz is carrying the Girl.
She puts her down.

Beatriz

You're going to have to run, sweetheart.
Look, you can almost see your dad from here.
He's just down the valley. See a shape in the trees?
Kid?
Please?

The Girl won't move.
She is being deliberately obstructive.

We don't have time for this.
You're going to have to run on your own feet. Fast.
Hold my hand, come on, let's go.

The Girl won't.
Beatriz kneels.

You want to reach him? Yes?

The Girl doesn't answer.
Beat.

What's your name?

Beat.

You must have a name?

The Girl doesn't speak.

Alright, whatever. Listen, we don't have long. I've got
to get back. You won't run, I could make you run.
I could pinch the backs of your knees like this –

Beatriz pinches her.

Go on then, run run run.

The Girl starts to cry.

OK.
OK, please – I didn't mean that. I'm sorry.

The Girl still cries.

Please stop.
I said I'm sorry. We just need to get moving.
Alright –
Get on my back, for God's sake.

The Girl starts to climb on Beatriz's back.

For crying out loud.
Ow, not like that, put your legs around me.
Are you made of stone or something?

A man, Rossignol, walks on.

Rossignol
Shush.

Beatriz
Who's that?

Rossignol

There are soldiers ahead, get down, what the hell are you doing?

Beatriz

I'm just trying to get this lump of a girl –

Rosignol

You can't go along here –

Beatriz

Why not?

Rossignol

They've blocked the crossing, won't let anyone past.

Beatriz

What crossing?

Rossignol

Keep her down, do you want to get us killed?

Beatriz

Why have they blocked it?

Rossignol

I don't know, you want to go and ask them?

Beatriz

I'm not scared of them, yesterday they were farmers.

Rossignol

Yes, but now they have pistols in their hands.

Beatriz

Pistols? They had pitchforks an hour ago.

She looks.

Did you see a man pass by?

Rossignol

Plenty.

Beatriz

He was just there, only
Small, pot-bellied, has a birthmark.

Rossignol

Not sure.

Beatriz

You wouldn't miss him.

Rossignol

Maybe.

Beatriz

I can't lose sight of him, he's so near.

Rossignol

Don't worry. He'll have been stopped too. No one
will get through this way until the morning.

Beatriz

Why are they stopping people?

Rossignol

I told you, they don't have to have a reason.
They're suspicious, jumpy,
Pumped up.

The Girl starts crying.

For God's sake shut her up.

Beatriz

I don't know anything about children.

Rossignol

Well, do something.

Beatriz

What do you suggest?

Rossignol

Pat her or hold her or something.

Beatriz
What?

Rossignol
Maybe she's thirsty.

Beatriz
Do you see any water?

Rossignol
I've got some.
Go on, take it, it's not poison.

Rossignol hands Beatriz a water bottle.
Beatriz gives it to the Girl.
The Child doesn't want it.
Rossignol gets out an apple.

Beatriz
I don't think that's going to work.

Rossignol
Try it.

Beatriz hands the apple to the Girl.
The Girl doesn't want it either.
Rossignol gets a small box out of his knapsack.
He opens the box and shows it to the Girl.
The Girl stops crying.

Beatriz
What is it?

Rossignol
A butterfly.

Beatriz
I know it's a butterfly, what sort?

Rossignol
A small fritillary butterfly, goes by the name of Melitaea.

Beatriz

It's pretty.

Rossignol

Are you a naturalist?

Beatriz

No, are you?

The butterfly flies away.

Don't do that, she'll cry again.

Rossignol

Then I'll show her another one
I've got a knapsack full of them.

He gets more small boxes out of his knapsack.
He hands one to the Girl.
The Girl is enrapt.

She looks frightened.

Beatriz

Well, don't look at me. I don't even know her name.
I thought I was doing her a favour, but she's difficult.
And I don't know anything about children, I'm not
even sure I like them.

Rossignol

Shush. She can hear you.

The Girl lets another butterfly go.

Listen, don't go along the path tonight. You'll get in
trouble. Wait here until morning, then take a short cut
across the river.
You'll catch him on the other side.

Beatriz

What river?

Rossignol

There's a river at the bottom of the valley.

Beatriz

I didn't know there was a river this way,
We've walked further than I thought.

Rossignol

Just a suggestion. Up to you.
I've got my own problems to deal with.

Rossignol gets a blanket out of his knapsack.
He rolls it up and puts it under his head.
Beatriz sits down.

Beatriz

I left my sister with twenty men. I was only supposed
to be a moment, two at most, and already –

Rossignol

Your girl's feet are blue.

Beatriz

She's not my girl.

Beat.

Rossignol

Do you want a blanket?

He gives it to her.

Beatriz

Don't try anything, I'm not that sort of woman.

Rossignol

I wouldn't have thought you were.

Beatriz takes it.
Beat.

You'd better tuck it around the both of you.

Beatriz looks at the Girl, then grudgingly tucks it round
her too.

Beatriz

Have you got anything to eat?

Rossignol

Yes, as it happens, do you want some?

Beat.
Beatriz shrugs. Not bothered.
Rossignol hands her an apricot.
And one for the Girl.
Beatriz takes both.

The second one is for her.

Beatriz passes it to the Girl.

You could say thank you.

Beatriz

What else have you got in there?

Rossignol

Everything you could need for the road.

He hands her another apricot.
They all eat.

What are you going to call her?

Beatriz

What do you mean?

Rossignol

You can't call her nothing.
All God's creatures have a name.

Beatriz

I'm not keeping her, I'm just delivering her to her
father, she's nothing to do with me.

Rossignol

Fine.

Beatriz

If I was to call her anything it would be stone or rock or lump.

Rossignol

Pebble.

Beatriz

That sounds too fond. And too light.
I don't really like children.

Rossignol

So you said.

Beatriz

I should have stayed at home.

Beat.

Where are you headed?

Rossignol

America. Three new species I'm hunting.

There is some kerfuffle in the bushes.

Beatriz

Did you hear that?

Rossignol

Shush.

They listen.

If you've brought the bloody soldiers –

Beatriz

Of course I haven't.

Rossignol

Just keep her quiet, get behind the bush.

Beatriz

It's a woman.

Rossignol
Shush.

Beatriz
She's covered in smoke.

A woman, Blandine, shouts.

Blandine
Someone help. Help the boy.

She is carrying a small Boy.
Both are on fire and covered in soot and smoke and burns.

It stings, help him.

Beatriz throws the water at the Boy.
Rossignol pats the flames out.

Rossignol
Is he OK?

Blandine
His mother had to run, his dad too,
He's still burning, the fire is out but his skin –

Beatriz wraps a blanket around her.

I have to get back, the rest of the village –

Beatriz
You can't go back.

Blandine
There are others injured.

The woman gets up to go.
Beatriz picks up the Boy to hand to her.

Beatriz
What about him?

Blandine
His parents have run, he won't see them again.

Beatriz

We can't keep him.

Blandine

Do what you can.

Beatriz

What do you mean?

Blandine

Leave him then, just don't give him to me.

The woman runs off.

Beatriz

What? Wait.
Now wait a minute –

Beatriz is left with the Boy.
She looks at Rossignol.

Well, are you going to run after her?

Rossignol

Do you want me to?

Beatriz

OF COURSE I DO!
Take the boy with you, go.

Rossignol picks the Boy up.

Rossignol

I won't catch her.

Beatriz

You could try.

Rossignol

He weighs a ton.

Beatriz

Bloody hell, try would you?

Rossignol

He's hot.

Beatriz

He just got burned. Run.

Rossignol

No, he is very hot. I think he has a fever.

Beat.
Beatriz puts her hand on his head.
Indeed he is hot.
Rossignol puts him back down.

Fourteen people died in my village last week.

Beatriz

You can't leave him.

Rossignol

If he has the same fever
Or worse there is some illness I've heard that is spread
by touch.

Beatriz

It could just be a little cough.

Rossignol

Putrid breath.

Beatriz

It's a little chill.

Rossignol

Fast pulse, I'm not risking it.
I've got to get to America.

Beatriz

To find an insect?

Rossignol

The fever. It digs inside your brain and it sends you
mad.

Beatriz

I can't carry them both,
I can't get her to her father, and him back to that
woman.

Rossignol

You should see the way they died, flailing around
and hallucinating.

Beatriz

Are you listening?

Rossignol picks up his blanket.
He takes the blanket off the Girl.
Puts them back in the knapsack.
Puts it on his back.

Rossignol

I'm a coward. I know I am.
What you're doing – it's amazing.

Beatriz

I'm a coward too.

Rossignol

No. Not like I am.
You're wonderful.

Beatriz

So help me.

Rossignol

I can't. Sorry. I know I'm a shit. I'm just a useless
lump of person. Everyone said I would come to
nothing. And you can't change me because I've always
been useless.

*He goes into his pocket. Gets out some money which he
gives to her.*

The short cut, keep walking, you'll get to a city with
a doctor.
That's a small fortune by the way, don't lose it.

Beatriz

I can't carry them both, didn't you hear?

Rossignol gives Beatriz a bag of something.

Rossignol

Sugar. You let her put her finger in and suck it every
so often if she walks, she'll walk.
When I said you were a really amazing woman,
I meant it.
I've got to go.

He comes back.
He gives her his knapsack.

In fact take the bag, it's got everything you could need.
Everything I have.

He runs.

Beatriz

Wait.

Beatriz is left with two small children.
She props the Boy up against a tree.

I'm sorry, it won't work. If I stop to get you to the
doctor, we'll never catch up with her father. And she
was here first.
I'll tuck the money in your shirt. If I could carry two
but . . .
Sorry.

She leaves the Boy, regretfully.
She takes the Girl's hand and walks away.
The Boy is left alone on stage.
Pause.

The Boy looks about, afraid.
Another pause.
Beatriz comes back in.

Oh, for God's sake then.

She picks him up and carries him, still with the Girl.

Just provided you know I'm no soft touch. Not one bit.
Both of you need to know that.

She walks off with both of them.

THREE
HUNGER

A city in France.
The city is different to anything Beatriz has seen. Skirts
are shorter, people harsher and there is the faded allure
of old advertising billboards all around. A motorised
bicycle is propped against an empty news stand, litter
and rats furnish the streets.
Beatriz and the children arrive at the door of a house.
Beatriz puts the children down.

Beatriz
Stop shivering.
If you can. And keep that tucked around you.

She rings the bell.

Look, put your hand under your chin, and wipe your
head on your sleeve. No one is going to die on me.

She rings the bell again.
No answer.
She bangs on the door.
Hard.

Answer the door or I will fucking kick it down.

A voice is heard from inside the house.

Madame
Who is it?

Beatriz
It's an emergency.

Beatriz starts to shiver too.
She turns around to the children.

It's OK, they are coming.
The doctor will sort us, then you'll be right as rain
and then over that hill and back in your village and
you back with your father and I'll get home to Rosa
by sometime tomorrow and hopefully the soldiers will
have left and the French will be out and everything
will be OK –

A woman comes to the door.

Madame
This better be good.

Beatriz
I need some help.

Madame
We all need help.

Beatriz
I was told a doctor lived here.

Madame
So?

Beatriz
I don't know this city, are you the doctor's wife?

Madame
You got money on you? You look nice and fat, you
come from somewhere wealthy?

Beatriz

I come from back there – we –

Madame

I'm not waking him, until I see what you are offering.

Beatriz

The boy needs help.

Madame

They all say that. But medicine is expensive and we
all need something to feather our caps.

Beatriz gets out some money.

Beatriz

Look.

Madame

Don't make me laugh.

Beatriz

It's a small fortune.

Madame

It's not worth the paper it's printed on.
Yesterday's money, where did you get that?

Beatriz

The boy has a fever.

Madame

Don't put it away, I didn't say I wouldn't take it.
It's just his fee is four times that.

Beatriz

I haven't got anything else.

Madame

Too bad then.

The woman is about to shut the door.

Beatriz

I won't move, I'll still be here in the morning.

Madame

We have gendarmes, they move people like you on.
We might be under siege but –

Beatriz

Siege?

Madame

Don't tell me you didn't notice.

Beatriz

Is there no part of you I can appeal to?

Madame

Yes, my belly.

Beatriz goes into the knapsack.

Pot of gold at the bottom, is there?

Beatriz gets out the contents.

Beatriz

Some apricots?

Madame

Nothing gets into the city for two months and you
just walk through the gates with a bag of apricots?

Beatriz

I need to see the doctor.

Madame

Well, that is just what we are considering.

Beatriz hands them over.

Halfway.

Beatriz

He is dying.

Madame

What else have you got in that bag?

Beatriz starts rummaging in Rossignol's rucksack.

Beatriz

Some boxes, a pocket magnifying glass, a moth trap, some blankets.

Madame

What's that?

Beatriz

A compass.

Madame

I'll take your boots.

Beatriz

My boots?

Madame

Final offer.

Beatriz

If I give you my boots I'll die.

Madame

It's a definite possibility.

Beatriz starts taking her boots off.

Beatriz

You would see me die?

Madame

We're all headed that way in the end.

She passes one boot to the woman.

Beatriz

Please be quick. I don't think the boy has all that long.

Madame

Both boots first.

Beatriz
Then your husband will come down?

Madame
Yes.

Beatriz passes the other boot over.
The woman picks them up and smells them.

Ouf – there's the cow.

Beatriz picks up the Boy.

Put him on the chair.

Beatriz puts him on the chair.
The woman looks at the Boy.

Beatriz
What about your husband?

Madame
I do the preliminary assessment.

Beatriz
What does that mean?

The woman lifts the Boy's eyelids. Checks his pulse.

Madame
It means, I'm sorry,
We can't help this one.

Beatriz
I just paid you.

Madame
Nothing I can do, as I thought.

Beatriz
What?

Madame
Right on the edge, poised towards the Almighty.

Beatriz

You aren't even going to try.

Madame

Hardly any pulse, weak in breath. You want to feel?
Oh, he's still warm, but that will pass.
No point waking the doctor to tell you the boy is
dead, unless you want a death certificate, but that is
more, and if you want a frame, well –

Beatriz looks at the Boy.

Beatriz

He isn't dead.

Madame

He will be soon.

The woman touches Beatriz's arm, softly.
Beatriz knocks her away.

Beatriz

You wasted time.
We were standing here talking about the fee for ten
minutes.

Madame

He was grave fodder from the second he caught that
fever. And she'll be the same if she's caught it off him.
The three of you in the earth by the end of the week.
I've seen it before, whole families going the same way.
Medicated pastilles only thing that you could try, but
even then –

Beatriz

Give me the pastilles then.

Madame

They're dear.

Beatriz

I JUST PAID YOU.

Madame

And I treated him. You paid for him.

Beatriz

You did nothing.

Madame

There was nothing I could do, was that my fault? You brought him to me as the patient. Is the physician responsible for the state of the patient before he walks into the surgery?

Beatriz

Give me my boots back.

Madame

They're my dinner now.

Beatriz

You're a thief.

Madame

So ring a bell.

She laughs.
Beatriz pushes her.
She pushes Beatriz back.
Beatriz hits out, the woman hits out.
The Girl bites the woman's ankles hard.
She screams.
The Girl bites harder.
Beatriz laughs.

Get her off me. Call your bloody dog off me, or I'll give her such a hiding.

Beatriz

I don't even know her name.
How can I call her off you?

The woman eventually gets the Girl off.
She picks up a stick.

Madame

You're going to have the beating of your life.

She approaches the Girl.

Beatriz

Don't you dare touch her.

Madame

I'll bloody do what I like.

The woman hits the Girl.
The Girl does nothing, doesn't even flinch.
The woman hits her again.
And again.
The Girl does nothing. It's Beatriz that screams.

Beatriz

Stop.

The woman hits her again.
The woman drops the stick.

Madame

She should be howling like a dog.
Why didn't that hurt her?

Beatriz

It did hurt her.

Madame

She didn't flinch.
The stick's hotter than she is.

Beatriz goes to comfort the Girl.

Beatriz

You barbarian.

Madame

Let me see her.

She grabs the Girl, looks at her all over.

There's no mark, no nothing.

She looks into her eyes.
The Girl breaks out of her grasp and picks up the Boy.

Her eyes are empty.

Beatriz
We're going.

Madame
She's like a statue, a painting, one of those creepy
ones whose eyes, now wait a minute, I know I haven't
played by the rules, but she – tell her not to curse me.

Beatriz
She's a girl.

Madame
If that's what she's thinking, because curses – tell her
to take it back,
Take it back, before it's done its damage.

She takes the boots off.

Look, I'll give it all back, with double, I'll throw in
some extra pastilles for interest.

She throws the blankets back, gives the money back to
the Girl.

I'll do anything, just
get her to take her black prayer away.

Beatriz and the Girl look a bit bemused.

I didn't mean it, you hear me. I am not myself, none
of us are when we are hungry like this.
Tell her, take it back.

Beatriz and the children walk on.
The woman throws stuff after them.

Take it back!

FOUR
BULLETS AND BARBED WIRE

Northern France.
Flat and full of mud.
Beatriz and the children trundle across a patch of land,
with very little sign of life in either direction.
The mud is thick and progress difficult.
The Girl holds a map.
She looks at it, and Beatriz looks at it.
Beatriz puts it away, and starts to walk on.
They hear the rattle of a gun.
They're frightened and duck.
They have no idea what it was.
Another one sounds and bullets go past.
This is an extremely hostile place and Beatriz wants to
get the children out of there as quickly as possible.
She comes across some barbed wire.
She doesn't know how to get across it.
She lifts the children across one by one.
Finally she hitches her skirt and climbs across herself.
More gunfire.
They all squat against each other, terrified.
A soldier runs on.
He lies down in the ground and starts to shoot.
He's rather too near Beatriz for her liking.
Beatriz and the kids sit still.
The soldier is shot right in front of them.
Beatriz puts her hands over the children's eyes.
More bullets.
They duck, make themselves as small as possible.
Beatriz holds the kids' hands and together they crawl on.
A young woman shouts.
She is tangled in the barbed wire, and almost entirely
covered in mud.

Beatriz doesn't want to stop.
The woman shouts again.
She has a baby with her, and needs help.
Beatriz tries to step over her.
The woman manages to get the Girl to take the baby.
The Girl starts to carry it.
Beatriz takes the baby off the Girl, and gives it back to the woman.
They can't help.
Beatriz leads the children away.
The woman shouts again, she is trapped and in terrible pain.
The Boy is standing by the woman, staring.
The woman gives the baby to the Boy.
Beatriz takes the baby from the Boy and goes back to give it back to the woman.
They have to get on.
A massive explosion. More bullets, crossfire.
They all cower for a second.
Beatriz is still holding the baby.
The baby cries.
The woman has been killed.
Her face is covered in blood, her scalp almost hanging off.
There is a pause in the fighting for just a second.
Beatriz looks at the baby.

Beatriz

Fucking hell.

Fucking fucking fucking hell.

She signals to the Boy.

Give me your belt, I'm going to have to strap her to my back.

The Boy passes his belt.
Beatriz straps the baby to her back.
The machine guns start up again.

FIVE

A square in a little town.
The Girl is sitting in the sun. The baby and the Boy are
beside her.
She sees something on the ground.
A butterfly.
She carefully goes into Rossignol's satchel and gets out
a box.
She catches the butterfly.
She looks at it.
She lets it go.
She tears a piece of paper into the shape of a butterfly.
She holds it up.
The Boy and the baby laugh.
She makes it flutter.
They laugh some more.
She lets it go.
It flutters to the floor.
She picks it up, she makes it flap.
Beatriz comes back.

Beatriz
I've got an address. Someone definitely saw a man
with a pot belly and a birthmark walk this way – not
three hours ago, we could still catch him. Plus, and
here's the clever thing. There's a train. He's walking,
but we get the train, hmm? Good, eh? We'll be waiting
for him in the next town?
Aren't you pleased?

The Girl looks up.

Tonight, you'll see him again. Imagine. Then we get
the others back to their homes.

Pause.

Don't you ever speak?
Any of you?

The Girl sees another butterfly.
She gets out the box.
She goes over to it.

I don't mind, but others might, that's all I am saying.
It could be seen as a bit rude. I've carried you all
halfway across the country after all, left my sister with
soldiers, just about broken my back.
A smile isn't that much to ask for, even if a word is
beyond you?

The Girl smiles.

So you understand then.
We'll pull your hair back, try to get the worst of the
mud off your legs. And when you see him, it'll be like
Easter or your birthday or one of those really special
days. He'll hug you tight and you'll feel like there was
nowhere in the world that you'd rather be. Even the
smell of his sweat, or the way his bristle feels on your
cheek, these are the things about dads that you miss
when they've gone. You lucky girl. And we'll all cry
and thank God or Spain or whoever.
Maybe he'll be so grateful he'll take these two too.

Beatriz takes the money out of the purse.
She counts it over.

And I'll go home.
Thankfully. I'll see Rosa. She'll be fine.
France will be gone, we'll have a wedding.
Hooray.

She smiles.

Have you ever been on a train?
I know you understand, so please an answer?

The Girl shakes her head.

What about you?

The Boy shakes his head.

Me neither. Saw a picture of one but –
We'll have to pretend we are posh.
We will be posh.
Madame Creole can fucking eat her heart out when
she hears.

She stops, she counts again.

What's happened?
We had three notes, where's the other one?

She looks at the Girl. The Girl says nothing.
She looks at the Boy.

Has anyone touched the bag, or been here?

Beat.
Beatriz tears through Rossignol's rucksack, taking
everything out.

We need that money for the train.
Oh God.

Everything comes out, boxes, apricots.
Beatriz is desperate.

It must be here, we had it before.

She can't find it.
The Boy brings over the paper butterfly.
He shows her.
Pause.

You fucking idiot. If we don't get that train – what
the hell were you thinking? This is money, you must
know the difference, I know you aren't as stupid as
you try to seem. For God's sake?
What the hell use is that?

Beatriz grabs him by the collar, shakes him.

I can't believe you did that? The train was our last
chance, don't you see? You think I want to be doing
this? You think I will have endless patience? I want to
see the back of you, don't you understand, finding her
father is the only hope for her, and you, and for me,
I have a life to get on with.
You bloody moronic lump of shit.
Christ.

She kicks the knapsack.

All of you. You're all morons.

She sits down, puts her head in her hands.
The Boy looks a bit lost.

Come and sit down next to her.

He puts an arm on hers.
Beatriz shrugs it off.

I don't know what the hell you'd do, if I were to say
you're on your own.
I'm tempted to do that, you know. I am tempted to
bloody well leave you here. All of you.

Beatriz sits with her head in her hands. The children sit
next to her. Awkward.
The Girl plays with the butterfly.
A soldier, Jacques, comes in.
He looks shy and bashful.
He approaches.

Jacques
They say back there, you're a mirage.

Beatriz ignores him.

Say you don't exist, says it's frightened soldiers seeing
something that isn't there.

Beatriz

Do you know you aren't making sense?

Jacques

But I say I don't care if you're all in my head, all I'm wanting is something in my head.

Beatriz

We haven't got anything.

Jacques

You walked right across the no man's land.

Beatriz

We had a long way to go.

Jacques

Do you know how scared we are?

We shake at night in case we're told to walk out there. We never sleep.

We shit ourselves, grown men. We can't control our shit, and every day we wake up and think today is the day, oh Jesus Mother Mary of Christ and All the Saints, today is the day.

Beatriz

Are you sure you're talking to me?

Jacques

Help me.

Beatriz

I've got my own problems.

Jacques

I need something to hold on to.

I need a little miracle.

Beatriz

There's no miracle here.

Jacques

You walked right across the wire
And you're still standing.

Beat.

Beatriz

I don't know what you want, and whatever it is, I'm
not that sort of person.

Jacques

I've got a bullet in my side.

Beatriz

I'm not a doctor either.

Jacques

You're a woman, aren't you, you've got a gentle hand.
Pull the bullet out.

Beatriz

Just because I'm a woman doesn't mean I'm bloody
soft, will help any bleeding heart.

Jacques

If you don't get the bits out next time the gas comes
I won't be able to run, and I'll stay stuck in my own
shit and my eyes will bulge and my insides will bleed
and mix with the shit.

Beatriz

What gas?

Jacques

The German gas.

Beatriz

German?

Jacques

I want to see my wife again, please.

Beatriz

I can't help you, I told you. I'm nothing. I'm just a woman with three kids.

We only walked that way because we got lost.

Jacques

I've got tobacco.

Chocolate for the children.

Money.

If you want –

He shows her some notes.

There's nowhere to spend it but –

Beatriz

I need to get a train.

Jacques

Rip out the bullet?

Beatriz

I might kill you.

I don't know what I'm doing, I can tear up a bandage but –

Jacques

I'm going to die anyway, sooner or later.

Beatriz takes the money.
He rolls up his shirt. It's a mess.

Beatriz

Children, don't look, you don't need to see this.

Beatriz puts the children's hands over their eyes, makes sure they can't see.
She looks at the man's torso. It's bad.

Jacques

My wife makes madeleines. When the pain comes I can smell the butter, she uses a whole cup of butter –

Beatriz
Listen, I only really know about goats.

Beatriz starts to try to pull the bullet out.

Jacques
And when the butter mixes with the egg, it's good, it's good.

He shouts in pain.

Beatriz
Sorry.

Jacques
No it's just – argghh.

Beatriz
You've got infection in the wound.

Jacques
Fucking hell, and the sugar goes on top.

Beatriz
Maybe I should stop.

Jacques
No, keep going, do it.

Beatriz
I can't get it, I don't have anything.

Jacques
I want to taste those cakes again. Jesus.

Beatriz tries. He shouts harder.
A second soldier comes on, Pierre.

It's not a fucking spectator sport, fucking hell.

Pierre
You won't taste the cakes that way.

Jacques
What?

Pierre

That's not the one you want, it's the girl.

Jacques

Fuck's sake, don't stop.

Pierre

The girl saved the Général.

Beatriz

What Général?

Pierre

Her shoe brushed past his sleeve and he woke up.

Beatriz

What are you talking about?

Pierre

He was out there for three days, half his blood on the grass.
Then he sits up and staggers back.

Beatriz

She's just a kid.

Pierre

A miracle. That's what we want. Like she did before.

Beatriz

Her?

Pierre

He'll pay double, whatever he has. And me, you can have my whole fortune if she cures my foot, and see these scabs –

Beatriz

Double?

Pierre

His wife makes madeleines, mine smells of lavender between her legs.

Beat.

Beatriz
You're mistaken.
She's just a child, she isn't –

Pierre
Then that's our folly.

Pierre gives her all the money he has.
Beatriz takes the Girl's hands away from her eyes.

Beatriz
Don't look.
Well, look and don't look.
Look for long enough to take the little pieces out,
then forget it.

She hands her the bandages.

We need the money for the train, you understand. It's
for you.
Imagine he's a goat –
Maybe your father keeps goats,
So you know about goats.
He's just a goat that got caught on a fence.

The Girl looks a bit paralysed.
Beatriz pulls the Girl out of earshot.

Look, I don't like this any more than you do, but if we
can get twice the amount, you see my thinking? We
can get that train, and catch your father. They think
you are some kind of miracle, so be a miracle. They're
stupid. It's easy. You saw what I did, you pull that
bullet out with your fingers, flesh is all the same, cow
or chicken. And when you've got the bullet out, and
we get to your father, we'll tell him what you did
and he'll be so proud, yes.

Jacques
Is she going to help us?

Beatriz

Yes she is. Aren't you?

The Girl takes the bandage.
She nods.

Good girl.

SIX

ACCUSATION

A clearing, outside the city of Metz.
The children are wearing military coats from the soldiers,
and the Girl is wearing a hat. Beatriz has a basin of
water, and is taking the clothes off the children to give
them a wash.

Beatriz

Really really clean.
It's so long since you've been clean I've forgotten
what colour your skin is.

They giggle as she flicks some water at them.
She takes out some soap, like a magician.

Look what we got from the soldiers.
I want you clean so when your father sees you
Da-duh.
I bet no one has ever seen this before.
Or knows what it's called. Anyone?
It's called soap.
Not to be confused with soup.
Soup is brown and sludgy and tastes of cabbage,
whereas this –

She tastes it.
She spits it out.
The children laugh.

Soap is not to be eaten.

They giggle some more.
She rubs it between her hands and makes bubbles.

And we got some sausage for supper.
And cheese and a blanket for the night and all on top
of the price of four tickets. We're on our way.

She blows the bubbles.

And it's supposed to smell like aloe vera, whatever
that is.

The children giggle even more.
Then she starts washing them.

And dads like clean little girls, they don't come back
if they are dirty, that's what my mother used to say.
Clean clean clean and your da you'll be seein'.
Tonight with any luck. Now arms up.
Now turn around.

She cleans the Girl's face.

What's wrong with your eye – it's all red. If it's soap
wash it out
Well wash it again
And again.

A stout German woman, Hanna, has been watching
Beatriz. She is with her teenage son.

Hanna
Suppose you think you can wash them and make them
good.

Beatriz
Hello?

Hanna
Too much bad on that big one, you'll never wash it off.

Beatriz
Are you talking to me?

Hanna

Your girl broke my son's arm when he was on his bike
for no reason.

Beatriz

Who did?

Hanna

Her.
That big one.

Beatriz

When?

Hanna

Today, earlier. When they were playing.
Show her.

Hanna's son is reluctant.

Don't worry, she can't hurt you now. She hurts you,
I'll break her neck.

Beatriz

She wouldn't hurt anyone –

Hanna

So who's done this then?

Her son stands forward.
Hanna shows Beatriz.
Indeed the arm is broken.

Beatriz

She's half his size.

Hanna

You'd better ask her.

Beatriz

It's ridiculous.

Hanna

Ask her.

Beatriz
Alright. Was this you?

The Girl says nothing.

See, innocent.

Hanna
You have to ask her harder than that.
You have to ask her with the back of your hand.

Beatriz
Have you done this?

The Girl comes over.

Hanna
Course she has, her silence says it all.

Beatriz
She's a good girl, I haven't had any trouble from her.

Hanna
She's a minx.
Rudi in the last village said she killed a goat.

Beatriz
I think you've got the wrong child.
She looks after the little ones, she sings them to sleep.

Hanna
Well, this arm didn't break itself.

Beatriz takes the Girl by the hand.

Beatriz
Truthfully. Is this something that you have done?

The Girl shakes her head.

Hanna
She's got you fooled.
She needs a thrashing, that's what.
Give me your belt, we'll do it ourselves.

Beatriz

You get away from her.

Hanna

You're spoiling her,
And the others.

Beatriz

Get away from all of us.

Hanna

They all say it, everyone in the village, sooner you
and your brat pass through the better.

Beatriz

That's not what they say.

Hanna

The soldiers maybe, the horny ones –

Beatriz

You take that back.

Hanna

Going to make me?

Beatriz picks up the brush.
Hanna laughs.

Beatriz

I'll chuck the water at you.

Hanna laughs and laughs.
She goads Beatriz, who picks up the basin.
Beatriz throws it.
She misses.
Hanna laughs again.

Hanna

You have me shaking in my boots.
Come on, let's go.

She and her son go.
Beatriz puts the brush down.

She holds the Girl.

Beatriz
You couldn't have hurt that boy, could you?

The Girl shakes her head.

You sure?

The Girl nods.
The Girl walks back to the other kids.
They move slightly further away from her.
The Girl picks up the sponge, they cower.

Why are you doing that?
Why are you moving further away from her?

The little ones say nothing.

You haven't hurt them, have you?

The Girl shakes her head again.

Then why won't they stand near you? Stand near each
other.
All stand together.
Us four, we're a team. We're all we've got.

The little ones won't move.

You. Take a step nearer to them.

She does.
One of the little ones weeps.

What is it?

The Girl kisses both of the other children.
Puts her arm around them.

That's it. We're one team.

Beatriz stands back.

And listen, the fighting has stopped.

Silence. Briefly.

SEVEN
TRAINS

Central Europe.
Beatriz and the children walk along the rails of the
railway track.
They are dressed in finery now, fur coats and hats made
of mink with scarves around their necks, and trailing
belts.
They are dragging a large suitcase and a couple of army
folding chairs; an umbrella; an empty birdcage; some
books; a lamp.

Beatriz

I don't see the point in printing a timetable. Don't
trail behind please, keep walking.

When we get to the next town you can do your trick
and we'll both get new shoes. And yes, some eye
ointment. And a waterproof for the rain.

An aeroplane flies overhead.
They duck.
Then stand and watch it.

I don't even know which way is north any more.
I thought the line went east to west but the sun –

The Girl has picked something up.
She brings it over. It's a shoe.

It won't fit me.

The Girl tries it on.
The Boy tries it on.

It'd be OK if you could find the other one.

The Girl runs back.

We can't go backwards, not a single step.

The Girl has gone, a little out of sight.

For God's sake!
I wish you had a name, then I could call you –
Well, you, you stay here.

The Boy runs back as well.

Come back, both of you.
For crying out loud. Alright, go, but don't go far. I'm
watching you
(*To the Baby.*) And don't you even think about it.

The children are out of sight.
Beatriz puts up a small army folding chair.
She sits on it.
The baby on her knee.
Looks at the sun. It's hot, hurts her eyes.
The baby cries.
She goes into Rossignol's knapsack.
She gets out an apricot.
She spits it out. It's bad.
She finds a biscuit.
She gives the biscuit to the baby who sucks it.
She takes out the bottle of water and drinks.
Euggh. That is bad as well.
She uses it on her feet.
She gets out something else from his knapsack. Some
sunglasses.
She puts them on.
Perfect.
Another aeroplane overhead.
She takes off the sunglasses to look at it.
A man, Jozka, comes in.

Jozka
You got tickets?

Beatriz
Is that a joke?

Jozka

I'm the ticket collector.

Beatriz just looks at him.

Don't say it, don't even dream of saying it.

Beatriz

There's no train.

Jozka

Hsst. Why would you say that?
Shhst. Just upsets everyone. Sorry, ma'am, she wasn't
thinking. And you, yes. No train? Only the Great
Trans-Europe Express.
Collected the tickets along this track every day for
sixty years.
Have you got a ticket or not?

Beat.

Beatriz

I've got an apricot.

Jozka

That'll do.

Beatriz

It's bad.

She offers him one.

Jozka

First stationmaster. Promoted every year for twelve
years. Three awards from the train company. Did you
want some help with your luggage?
Get your children on OK?

Beat.

Beatriz

I don't know what to say to you –

Jozka

Say yes, and that you'd like it stacked careful because it is full of fragile items, and would I be so kind as to move the heavy one first so it isn't against the door.

Beat.

There are trains, by the way.

Beatriz

I haven't seen a train in two weeks.

Jozka

They come at night, they use this line.
I lie in bed with the wife, hear people crying as the train goes past.
Taking them to God knows where.
I can move you up to First Class if you like?

Beat.

Said they don't need me any more
Get the best view from the seat in the first carriage.
Luggage on top. Little lamps by the window. Doors that open out.

He eats the apricot.

Euggh.

Beatriz

I told you.

The Girl comes back in. She has collected an armful of shoes.
She puts them down.
The Boy, the same.
A huge pile of abandoned shoes.
There is nothing to say, really.
The Girl starts rummaging through them.
Beatriz stops her.

Don't.

I'm sorry, when her eyes are sore she doesn't see so well. Stop it.

Beat.

Jozka

Let me move you up to First Class, and I'll tell you something I know.

Beatriz

Are you crazy?

Jozka

There's whispers of you and the girl all up and down this line. Some of the people in the trucks say if they see the girl they'll get out OK. I say why not, if I was in their position I would hang on to something too. All you have to do is let me sell you a ticket. You don't have to buy it or anything, you just have to say you want one. And where you are going, and whether you want to sit by the window or with the riff-raff. Have you found the man you're looking for?

Beat.

The traitor?
You're famous, I told you. Everyone knows about the woman who carries the children on her back and won't stop her search until she's found the girl's father. Don't worry, you're admired, they think you're a little crazy but basically they're on your side.
They understand the girl needs to get back to her father, and you're like a camel.

Beatriz

Has he been this way?

Jozka

Buy a ticket.
Won't cost you much.

Beatriz
Where to?

Jozka
The end of the line.
Krakow one direction, Berlin the other.

Beatriz
Krakow.

Jozka
Beautiful place, you'll love it there.
Holiday, is it?

Beatriz
Has he passed through?

Jozka
You're not doing it right.

Beat.

Beatriz
Yes, a holiday. Me and the children.

Jozka
How long?

Beatriz
Two weeks.

Jozka
Over the bank holiday or coming home before?

Beatriz
Before.

Jozka
Nice. Could slip you a guide book for an extra coin
or two,
Mark the places you should visit?

Beatriz
No, thank you, no guide book.

Jozka puts down his ticket bag, looks at Beatriz.

Jozka
It's too late, anyway.

Beatriz
What?

Jozka
They could have told you in the last town,
You've missed him,
He's up for trial, might be shot tomorrow.

Beatriz
Why?

Jozka
Read for yourself.

He takes out a newspaper.

He talked to the enemy.

Beatriz
About grain.

Jozka
Not what it says here.
Got him holed up like an animal anyway by the time
you get there.

Beatriz
Where?

Jozka
Why do you care? He isn't your father. What is he
to you?

Beatriz
Which way?

Jozka
Aren't you tired now, aren't you really tired?

Beatriz

Are you listening?

Jozka

Yes, I'm listening, but we're not so different, you and me. We both keep going without asking whether we should. I know how you feel, I've got to sell that day's tickets, get my quota, because what do I do if I don't?

Beatriz

I played your game.

Jozka

It's terrifying.

Beatriz

Tell me which way.

Jozka

What would we do, if we don't?

Something starts rumbling in the distance, a bell rings.

That's a plane, get the children off the line, the bombs are coming.

Beatriz

Which way?

Jozka

East.

Beatriz

Which way is that?

Jozka

That way –
Wait, wait.
I'll give you a gold korona if she can bring the real trains back.
Make the war stop. Two even. You can have everything I have for the trains to start properly again. Could she do that?

Beatriz takes the gold coin.
She smiles at Jozka as she puts it in her pocket.

Beatriz
    Of course she can.

Beatriz starts to walk, the children follow.
The planes fly overhead.

EIGHT
INTIMIDATION

Inside a prison building.
Beatriz and the children arrive.
This feels more modern now.
A Vietnamese woman, Thi, comes in and watches them.

Thi
    Where she trod it's said the ginger roots are already
    growing.

Beatriz
    I need to speak to the officer in charge.

Thi
    The mint has started to flower.

Beatriz
    It's really urgent.

Beatriz rings the bell again.

Thi
    I've got a family who are starving, a boy who –

Beatriz
    I'm sorry, I don't mean to be rude.

Thi
    Doesn't play, his ribs –

Beatriz

But would you just listen!
We're here to try to save a man.

Thi

Here? You can't save anyone here.

Beatriz

Her father is being held.

Thi

Good luck to him.

Beatriz

How do you get attention?

Thi

The Americans kill everything we have, they have a
spray –
The trees die, the children die, the ground –

Beatriz rings the bell again.

You're just like them –
You don't care,
Maybe you chew the same gum.

The Girl goes over to Thi, touches her scarf.

Beatriz

Don't do that.

Thi

She's full of goodness.

Beatriz

I said there wasn't time.

Thi

Do you want money?

Beatriz

I want to be seen, that's what I want, to ring this bell,
and someone to come, and to find her father, and then
to go home.
That's all I've wanted.

She rings the bell.

Thi

We're disappearing. We'll be dead soon.
We hear about this girl, can make the crops grow.
Now I see you don't care, you just want to get fat.

Beatriz

That isn't true.

No one is coming.

Thi

They won't come. by the way.
You can ring all day, they won't come.

Beatriz

How do you get them to come?

Thi

You say you have names.
You shout 'Charlie coming, I got names.'

Beatriz

What names?

Thi

Just a little dance, a little tread,
Then the ginger will grow again, maybe the papaya.

Beatriz realises she needs this woman's help.

Beatriz

Alright, how far is this field?

Thi

It's here outside the doorway.
They built this where our food used to grow.

She only has to step outside the door –

Beatriz

She needs to stay clean, I don't want her to get dirty.

Thi

If there's shit it's from the Americans.

Beatriz

She can't get shit on her legs.

Have you got something she can wrap around her?

Thi

Only my scarf.

Beatriz

That will do, come here.

Thi

It was a wedding present.

Beatriz

I've carried her around a thousand miles to find her father – she's not going to see him with shit all over her legs.

Thi

My husband gave it to me on our first night.

Beatriz

Do you want her help or not?

Thi takes her scarf off.

I don't mean to be unreasonable,
I'm tired, that's all, and hungry.
Have you got any apricots?

Thi

Not really, a last cup of rice saved for –

Beatriz

Rice then.
And something to drink?

Thi

My husband found a coconut.

Beatriz

Coconut, yes, good. We like coconut.
And some milk for the baby.

Beat.

And be quick,
I want her back quickly.
But first tell me which window do I knock on, what
secrets do I tell them?

Thi

You ring the other bell.

Thi shows her a buzzer.
She goes off with the Girl.
Beatriz rings the buzzer.
An American marine, Hancock, appears.

Hancock

If you're armed lay them down.

Beatriz

I've got nothing.

Hancock

Put your hands behind your head.

Beatriz does so.
Hancock comes right up to her.

Do you know what you're in the middle of?

Beatriz

We've come about a man you are holding.

Hancock

We're holding lots of people, little lady.

Beatriz

He has a birthmark on his face, and a belly that sticks out and his father was French.

Hancock

A gook?

Beatriz

I said French.

Hancock

You're pretty tough.

Beatriz

My name is Beatriz.

Hancock

Is that so?

Beatriz

And I'm travelling with his daughter.

Hancock

Someone sent you?
Are you here to check on us?

Beatriz

No, we sent ourselves.

Hancock

I should pass you in front of the intelligence officer, see what he makes of you.

Beatriz

Is he around?

Hancock

Are you a lawyer?

Beatriz

We just want to see your prisoner.

Hancock

A journalist then?

Beatriz
Why would I be a journalist?

Hancock
Don't play games with me, this is a war we are fighting. These Cong, they –

Another man, Glennister, comes out.

Glennister
Hancock, get back in there, those guys they –

Hancock
I'm just dealing with a situation, sir.

Glennister
Another situation?

Beatriz
My name is Beatriz.

Hancock
I think she's Press.

Beat.

Glennister
Get her a chair, then.

Beatriz
I want to see a man –

Glennister
Pass me a towel, would you? I want to wipe my hands. Pleased to meet you.

Beatriz
I understand you're holding him.

Glennister
A detainee?

Beatriz
Yes.

Glennister

It's a clean situation around here. No funny business.

Hancock

Everyone treated with utmost respect.

Glennister

We find if we treat the gooks well, the words they just tumble out of them. Names, places, they just –

Hancock

Trip off the tongue.

Glennister

Exactly.
We give them a hot bath.

Hancock

Not too hot.

Glennister

Something for their stomachs.

Hancock

Something nice for their stomachs.

Glennister

Do you want to write this down, tell the folks back home?
Get her a pencil, or better, bring in a camera.

Hancock

Here.

Glennister

Every cell has space to move around, a view of the outside.
Hell, we'd fit television aerials if we could afford it.

Beatriz

Most of all we'd like to see him.

Beat.
Glennister laughs.

Glennister
See him?

He laughs again.

See him?
Who did you say you write for?

Beatriz
I didn't say.

Glennister
You want to play games?

Beatriz
I've walked a long way.

Glennister
This is a war, Miss . . . what was your name?
We have to do what we have to do.
You understand that?

Beatriz
What does that mean?

Glennister
What do you think it means?
What's his name, your guy?

Beatriz
Colline.
He has a birthmark.

Glennister
Here?

Beatriz
Yes.

Glennister
Is it the same guy?

Hancock shrugs.

So let's get him out here.

Hancock
Sir, I –

Glennister
No, let's show the reality to the folks back home.
They send the journalists because they want to know.

Hancock
Are you sure, sir?

Glennister
Let's let this lady and her paper have a look.
This is what we do with people that fuck with us.

Beatriz
Oh God, you've killed him.

Glennister
Not officially. He still has a pulse.

Hancock brings out a man in a wheelchair, with his head covered.
It's horrible.
Beatriz covers the children's eyes.

When you fuck with us, you fuck with the devil.

Beatriz looks at the man.

You want him?
You can take him away if you want.

Beatriz pulls back the cloth over his face.
It's a total mess.

Beatriz
Oh sweet Jesus.

The man falls off the wheelchair. Like an animal carcass.

Wake up.

Beatriz touches his face.

Wake up, it's over.

Glennister goads her, starts humming a tune.
Beatriz takes the soap out of her bag and tries to wash
off some of his blood.
Carefully, gently.

We'll take you back with us, take care of you,
Whoever you are.

Glennister laughs at the futility.

Glennister
You want some skin lotion to go with that?

Beatriz puts her finger to his pulse.
She lets out a sob.

Beatriz
He's dead.

Glennister
So ring a bell.

The Girl comes in.
She sees the man.
Beatriz looks at her.
The Girl looks at Beatriz.
Lost for a second.

Beatriz
Don't look.

The Girl doesn't move.
She still looks at Beatriz.
Beatriz tries to keep her from looking.

It's not even clear that it's him or not.
His face, you can't see –
Don't look.

The Girl does so.

This isn't your father, this is some unfortunate –
Just a man.

The Girl starts to pull at her eyes.

Don't scratch.

She scratches and scratches.

Stop, you'll hurt yourself.

Beatriz comes over to the Girl and tries to stop her.

Don't.

The Girl claws at her eyes.
She pushes Beatriz off.

You're making them bleed.
They're bleeding.
Stop it.
Stop it.

Beatriz manages to get both the Girl's arms and holds them by her side.

Stop it.

A Vietnamese farmer, Xuan, comes in, dragging Thi.

Xuan
Frauds.

Glennister
You want to take that back –

Xuan
The woman and the girl. Pretending to be something they're not.

Beatriz
Please leave us.

Xuan
Taking our food.

Glennister
This won't pass.

Xuan

All the women and men and children are in the field, singing and dancing, believing that all we have to do is dance and we'll be kept safe.

Glennister

What dancing?

Thi

Where she has trod the ginger root –

Xuan

You see how they are taken in?

Hancock

They can't dance, this is a war zone.

Xuan

And when they find out they've been lied to, they'll be angry.

Glennister

Angry?

Hancock

If they've jeopardised our location –

Glennister

Or worse, find out –

Xuan

Ask her if she took payment?

Beatriz

I asked for some rice.

Glennister

Get on the phone.

Xuan

Some fish, some coconut, she is even wearing my wife's scarf.

Glennister
If this gets out of hand –

Xuan
They're dancing like the girl is some kind of god,
a saviour.

Glennister
Leads to an uprising –

Beatriz
People wanted to believe.

Thi
I do believe it.

Hancock
What should I do, sir?

Xuan
In this place, we honour truth, peace, the law of life.
We don't like to be lied to.

Glennister
Wait a minute, who's lying?

Beatriz
I never lied.
If people believed, then that was because they –

Glennister
Believed what?

Beat.

Xuan
That the child has power, is miraculous.
Can cure the lame, heal the sick,
Bring back the ginger root from total devastation.

Beat.

Glennister
Is that what you said?

Beatriz
Not exactly.

Glennister
So what did you say?

Beat.

Beatriz
I feel a bit under pressure, could you stand back.

Glennister
ANSWER THE QUESTION!

Hancock
In law there's either the truth, or the mistruth.
Truth was your light bulb, not ours.

Beatriz says nothing.
Hancock slaps Beatriz across the face. Hard. It's shocking.

Glennister
It's easy.
Is the child miraculous? Yes or no?

Beatriz
. . .
Yes, then.
Sometimes.

Glennister
Sometimes?

Beatriz
Yes, sometimes.

Hancock
She'll have to prove it.
In our country, we need proof.

Xuan takes something from his wife. He brings out a dead bird in a clay pot.

He hands the pot to Beatriz.

Xuan

My wife had started to cook this for you.
She'd washed the lime leaves already, covered it in salt,
Put in some carrots.
If the girl is what you say she is, let's see her bring
the bird back to life.

Beat.

Beatriz

But she . . .

Glennister

She's either miraculous or she isn't.

Beatriz is still reeling from the slap.
She hands the bird and the pot to the Girl.

Bring the bird back to life.

The Girl looks at it.
She won't even pick it up.
The other children look at her.
Beatriz tries to get her to hold it.
It's useless.

Beatriz

It's too big a thing to ask for, magic isn't something
you can switch on like a tap, she needs –

Glennister

What does she need?

Xuan

More coconuts, more grilled fish?

Beatriz tries again.
She gets the Girl to hold the bird.
She looks around. Everyone is crowding in.

Beatriz

Can you give her a bit of space?

Glennister

She can have all the space she needs.

This isn't going to work.
Beatriz speaks to the Girl.

Beatriz

You're going to have to do something.
Anything.
They're all watching.

Xuan

She can't do it.

Glennister

You'll have to pay back everything you made.

Beatriz

It was survival, a way to feed the children.

Hancock

Every meal, every coin.

Beatriz

I can't do that.

Hancock

Then face a jail term with us.
A few days in the cell with the other men should see
the debt through.

Beatriz

You're barbaric.

Hancock

And lonely.

Hancock laughs.
Glennister comes towards her, ready to manhandle her.

Glennister

My turn first,
I love a lively bitch.

Thi screams.
She throws back her head and screams.

Hancock

What's wrong with the woman?

Thi speaks in Vietnamese.
Xuan shouts in Vietnamese to the people outside.

Xuan

Get the children in.

Glennister

What?

Xuan

Outside from the sky, planes.

Glennister

Damn it, get cover.
They attracted attention, that dancing.

Thi

The sky.

Xuan

It's American planes.

Glennister

We didn't send them.

Thi

The spray, the trees.

Glennister

Get on the phones – oi, stop.

Xuan is holding Thi.

Xuan
You can't go out.

Thi
Our boy is out there.

Hancock
I can't get through to them.

Glennister
Try again.

Xuan
You go out, you'll die.

Hancock
Why are they doing this?

Thi
He's burning.

She breaks free, runs.

Xuan
Thi –?

He runs after her.

Glennister
Shitting hell, each for his own.
Salvage what you can.

A siren sounds
*Mayhem and running. The sound of aeroplanes and fire
in the background.*
Other soldiers appear.
Everyone panicking, running, burning.
Beatriz and the children are in the middle of it.
They are entirely ignored.
They hang on to each other.
Eventually everyone else has gone.
They are alone.

Beatriz
Did you see that?

Beat.
Beatriz doesn't want to look.

The woman just now, running after
Her boy
She was here, just now –
Her skin –
Her skin peeled off her shoulders
And the boy –
Did you see?

The Girl is still holding the bird.
Silence.
The Girl opens her hands and the bird flies away.

NINE
DESECRATION

The oilfields of the desert, after everyone has gone.
Nothing much in either direction, only sand and bits of
old tarpaulin. Some twisted metal, and debris. A broken-
down tank.
Rossignol is holding a spade and digging a hole.
Behind him is a butterfly trap.
The Girl stumbles in.
She can't see.
She has a bandage round her head, over her eyes.
Blood has seeped through where the eyes should be.
She holds a broken and mangled semi-automatic gun.
She is dishevelled, dirty and in rags.
She sits down near to Rossignol.
She plays with the gun.
He doesn't notice her at first, then speaks.

Rossignol
Hello.

She doesn't acknowledge him.

I said hello.
Think you should put that down.
Some of them still work.

He continues to dig.

You can check the trap for more moths if you like.

The Girl does nothing.
She still plays with the gun.

Go on, I think I saw some fly in earlier.
See if we've got any pretty ones.

He stops digging.

What happened to your eyes?

She doesn't answer.
He opens his knapsack and gets out a nut.

Want an almond?
They aren't very fresh but –

He hands her one.
She can't see it to take it.
He puts it into her hand.
He eats one.
The Girl hands him a dead butterfly from her pocket.

There's no moisture in him. He's all dried up too, little
fellow.
You can put it in a box anyway if you want, or just
lay him down in the sand.

The Girl does nothing.

There's a box in my bag.
What happened to you?

The Boy comes in. Also filthy.
He looks at the hole.
He whistles.
The Girl pushes the Boy down the hole.

Hey.

He helps the Boy out.

That wasn't very nice.

The Girl shrugs.
She carries on playing with the gun.
Beatriz comes in, carrying the baby. She looks like she's
starving. Has nothing.

Beatriz
Stay away from them.
I might not look like much but –

Rossignol
I'm a friend.
You don't recognise me?

Beatriz
I'm very tired.

Rossignol
Rossignol.
We met on the road.

Beatriz
Did we?

Rossignol
I gave you some apricots.

Beatriz
Must have been a long time ago then. I don't
remember everyone we've met. We've met a lot of
people, too many mostly.

Rossignol

I gave you the knapsack.

Beatriz

Yeah well, it's empty now.

Rossignol

I'll have it back then.

Beat.
Beatriz keeps it.

Beatriz

Hey children, come back over here.

Rossignol

They're OK.

Beatriz

He wants to know what are you digging for?

Rossignol

Plant roots, I thought I might find moisture.
You're thirsty, aren't you?
You look thirsty.

Beatriz

Of course he is. We all are.
But I've told them there's no point. You dig, you use
up energy. You use up energy, it takes more water.
I heard you can only last forty days without drinking
something, and today we are on forty-one.

Rossignol

So God is smiling on you.

Beatriz

You think?

She laughs.

God, are you smiling up there? Is this a good joke
for you?

I've told him already, death would be OK if I don't
have to walk there.
We don't pee any more, we don't spit. Even our blood –

Rossignol
I've got an apricot.

Beatriz
Is it as dried up as me?

She eats it.

Rossignol
I came back for you. That night.

Beatriz
As I said, I can't remember you.

Rossignol
That's lucky. I was a coward,
I realised at the time, but anyway I want you to know
I did come back.

Beatriz
Well, it's all very interesting but a little academic.

Rossignol
It was the biggest mistake of my life if you want to
know.

Beatriz
Well, ring a bell.

Rossignol takes the shovel and starts digging.
The Girl feels around, and helps him.
Beatriz is amused.

She likes you.
She doesn't usually lift a finger.
Maybe she remembers you even if I don't.

Rossignol
She's grown.

Beatriz

They do that.

Beatriz sits down and watches them.
The Girl and Rossignol dig.
Rossignol watches the way the Girl stumbles around half blind.

She has an itch, her eyes –
I put a bandage around to stop her scratching, that's all.

Beat.

You know the only good thing about this thirst is the mirage that goes with it. Sure, mainly it's lakes and rivers and stuff like that, but sometimes it's people. This morning I saw my grandmother twice, and my father, he walked right over to me. And I can ask them, talk to them about the children. About her. Did I go wrong, I say. She hurts the others, she brings bad things, is that my doing?

Rossignol

No.

Beatriz

You're probably just another mirage. Arguing for the other side.
I don't know what she is sometimes. Fowl or fish, bird. Some creature. And I'm old. I'm at the end.
I found an old bit of tin foil and I looked at my face.
I'm really old. I've given my life to this.
It's day forty-one. God, what are you doing?

Rossignol

Do you want another apricot?

Beatriz

OK.

Beat.

What happened to America?
The missing species?

Rossignol
You remember me now.

Beatriz
It's coming back. When you used the word 'coward' it sort of fell into place.

Rossignol
I don't know about America. I got as far as the boat, then –
It was a folly, I thought there was nothing more important than insects.
I was crazy.
It was crazy.

Beatriz
Yeah, well, there's lot of it about.

Beat.
The Girl comes back in.
She is carrying something with a cloth over it, a jug.
She gives it to Rossignol.

You've made an impression on her.

Rossignol takes the cloth off.
The Girl takes the bandage off her eyes.

Rossignol
Where did you get this?

Beatriz
What is it?

He puts his finger in.

Rossignol
How on earth did you find this?

The Girl points.

Taste it.

The Girl produces a cup from out of her pocket, which she also gives to Rossignol.

How could she have got it?
A jug full?

Beatriz
I told you, she scares me sometimes.

Rossignol
The only well I know has a queue that takes a week
to get to the top.

He pours the water into the cup.
He drinks it.

Beatriz
Is it OK?

Rossignol
It's perfect.

Beatriz
It's not bad?

The Girl gets another cup out of her pocket and a third and a fourth.
Rossignol pours them all some water.
Beatriz takes hers.

Rossignol
You don't trust her?
It's delicious. Pure like a stream.

Beatriz drinks.
The Boy drinks.

You agree?

Beatriz

I agree.

Tastes almost like wine it's so good.

Rossignol

So let's get drunk.

I mean, would you mind getting drunk with me? I'd like to.

Beatriz gives some to the baby.

Beatriz

Some people used to say, a while ago, she could do things, I never believed them but –

Rossignol pours another glass.

Rossignol

She's a magician, aren't you?

Beatriz

Don't say that.

Rossignol

Why not?

I didn't say she was magic, I said she was a magician. Look.

Rossignol pulls a bunch of flowers from his sleeve.

For you.

The children laugh.
He gives them to Beatriz.

Beatriz

What's this?

Rossignol

You could say I made the flowers appear from thin air, or you could say I already had them up there waiting for the right woman.

Beatriz
The right woman?

The Girl pulls a long scarf from out of her bodice.

Rossignol
She's the same.
She knows the art.

He takes his shoe off.

See, nothing there.

*He taps it twice and lifts it. Underneath is a live frog.
The children gasp again.*

It looks like magic, but it's all tricks.

Beatriz
She made a bird come back to life.

Rossignol
So she had a live bird in her coat and she swapped it.

Beatriz
She fooled a crowd.
She healed some soldiers.

Rossignol
She's clever. Listen. There is nothing in the world that
is properly magic. Only nature. That's magic alright.
A baby growing in its mother's womb, a brown worm
that turns into a butterfly, a barren field that breaks
with flowers. You want to see something truly
miraculous? Look all around you. Look at the way
two people look at each other when they're in love.
The rest is just show, it's a trick.
There's nothing to fear in this girl.
Her father did the biggest disappearing trick of all,
and she is a magician's daughter.

The Girl takes an empty oil can. She taps it.

She shows them, it is completely solid.
Then she squeezes it. Out comes blood.

> Now let me see that. Very good, that is one I haven't
> seen before. Have you got something up your sleeve
> or have you cut yourself?

Rossignol catches her arm, tries to look.

> Can you show me how you did it?
> It's still bleeding, it's amazing.
> Let me into the secret.

She shakes her head.
Beatriz laughs.

> A magician's daughter indeed.
> Would you kiss me if I asked?

Beatriz
> Maybe.
> Are you asking?

Rossignol
> Maybe.
> Who's that?

Beatriz
> Where?

Rossignol
> Can you see someone?

Beatriz
> It's another mirage, don't worry.

A man walks on, Farshad, he is carrying a dead woman's
body.

Farshad
> It takes some gall to drink –

Rossignol
> He is still there.

Farshad

When I need a grave.

Beatriz

He'll go.

Farshad

Ask her, that piece of evil sitting beside you.

Beatriz

Don't talk to him if you want him to go quicker.

Farshad

I saw her go to the well, she passed me on the way.

Rossignol

He hasn't gone yet.

Beatriz

Neither he has.

Farshad

A queue snaking back a mile, everyone with their pots – no don't let her come near me. Stand back, ask her about it.

Beatriz

Ask her about what?

Farshad

My village. She killed my village, she twirled her scarves, she danced, she got them to do what she wanted. They thought she was an angel, some kind of god that would bring more water, they would have done anything for her. So she put her arms out like this, and they followed. And then another way, and then like this, her hands to her eyes, and they did the same. All of them, all ten thousand. And she put her fingers further in and so did they and further, and they tore. They tore and tore at their own eyes. They wanted water, they'd have done anything. They were desperate. And then when they could see nothing and were haemorrhaging into the sand she got them to lie down and stepped over them to fill her bottle. Go on, ask her.

Rossignol
Of course we'll ask her, we've nothing to fear.

The Girl gives them some more water.

Where did you get the water?

The Girl says nothing.

I bet she didn't even go to the well. I bet she found it somewhere else, she's a clever girl.

Beatriz
Where did you get it?

The Girl pulls down a bit of old tarpaulin and reveals some bodies.
The bodies are grotesque.
Eyes are indeed gouged out.
Beatriz covers the Boy's and the baby's eyes.

Rossignol
Oh my God.

Beatriz retches.
The Girl draws back another cloth and reveals some more.
Bloodied and terrible.

Beatriz
Get her to stop.

Farshad
She isn't even ashamed, look at her.
Have you raised her to know nothing?

Beatriz
Please get her to stop.

Farshad
Why did she do it, what did they ever do to her?

Rossignol
She was thirsty.

Farshad
WE ALL ARE.

The Girl reveals more bodies, more and more.
They are surrounded by the dead.

Beatriz
Oh God.

Farshad
First children bring bombs, now this.

Beatriz
PLEASE STOP!
Stop giving me water, STOP IT!

The Girl stops.
Beatriz gives the water back to the Girl.

I can't drink your water now.
I can't even look at you now.
Don't you know what I've done?

The Girl picks up the bandage that she had cast off
earlier.
She starts to wrap it round the Boy's head, covering his
eyes.

Farshad
I need to take her away.
We still have justice here.

Beatriz
What do I do now, huh? Have you got an answer for
this?

Rossignol

She's not a child any more, she's not your responsibility.

Beatriz

God, it's day forty-one. Please – enough.

She bats the Girl away from the Boy.

Don't touch him.

The man grabs the Girl by the shoulders.
She tries to struggle.

Farshad

They'll have to try her, punish her.

He punches her.
She submits.

Beatriz

Did you have to punch her like that? She would've
come, she –

Farshad starts to pick up a rope.
It's awful to watch, the Girl is like a felled animal.

Do we have to watch?

Farshad

She's your faecal waste.
Yes, you have to watch.

Farshad starts to tie the rope round the Girl.
The Girl is inert, defeated.
Rossignol tries to say something that is of comfort.

Rossignol

Sometimes in nature, sometimes you get a bad one,
a caterpillar turns yellow before it can make a pupa,
a kid that dies before it can drink milk. Even in nature
you get some individuals that will hurt others for no
reason other than –

The Boy stands up by the gun that the Girl was playing with.

Boy
BANG.

Beatriz
What are you doing?
Oh God, enough already.

The Boy aims the gun at Farshad.

Boy
BANG.

Beatriz
You're a good boy, what are you doing?

The Girl takes her scarf out, the one from Thi, and twirls it.

Boy
BANG.

Farshad
What's he doing?

Beatriz
I don't know.

Boy
BANG.

Farshad
Both of them, get them to stop.
Put the gun down. It isn't a toy.

Boy
BANG.

Farshad puts his hands up.

Farshad
OK, OK.

Boy
BANG.

Beatriz
They're just children.

Farshad
I've had enough.

Boy
BANG.

Farshad
STOP IT.

Farshad puts down the rope.

She's an animal, but she's free.

Boy
BANG.

Beatriz
Stop saying that.

The Girl steps out of the ropes.
The Boy is still holding the gun. He picks up the baby.

Boy
BANG.

Beatriz
Put the baby down.

The Girl twirls her scarf again. She puts her arms out.

Boy
BANG.

Beatriz
Give it back.

Farshad
Her first acolyte.

Beatriz
GIVE THE BABY BACK.

The Girl backs away.
Beatriz stands up, tries to grab the Boy, pleads with him.

There is something wrong with her, don't –

Boy
BANG.

Beatriz
Just give me the baby back.

Boy
BANG.

The children are backing away.

Beatriz
No no no.

Rossignol
What should I do? Should I do something?

Boy
BANG.

They have almost gone.

Beatriz
YES.
YOU SHOULD GO AFTER THEM.
YOU SHOULD GET THEM BACK.
YOU SHOULDN'T STOP UNTIL YOU GET THAT
BABY BACK.

Rossignol
Now I know.

Rossignol runs.
Farshad runs off behind him.
Beatriz is left alone with the dead.
Beat.
She looks around.

Beatriz
    Oh God.

*She looks towards the way the children left, we can still
hear the Boy saying 'Bang' in the distance.*

    Oh God.
    Oh God.
    Oh God.
    Oh God.
    This is a dream
    A mirage
    I'm dead already.

She pulls back some clothing to look more closely.

    Oh God.
    It's day forty-one.
    The world's gone crazy.

She puts the clothing back.

    Oh God.
    Twins,
    A pregnant woman,
    A young man,
    Fluff on his lip,
    An ancient,
    Ears drooping,
    A little one, still holding his water pot and hoping
    for a drink.

Beatriz is holding up the body of a woman.

    And this one,

And this one,
A bride perhaps.
Waiting for her wedding day.

She walks to the next body.

And you – perhaps the groom
You look –
Does everyone look the same, wherever you go?
You look just like Tomas.
I don't mind, you get blood on my dress.
Your face crumples in the same way that his did.
And you, sweetheart bride, you have the same pretty
hair.

She holds the two bodies close to her. They loll.

Tomas and Rosa written in the vines.
And if you are Tomas, and she is Rosa –
Then maybe –
Maybe that could be our tree there
And that could be our gate. There the stump we used
to tether the goat on.
The well could have been our well.

Beat.

Home?
Could I be home . . .?

She cradles the dead body.
The dead woman's body starts to writhe.
She's covered in blood.
Beatriz drops her.

Uggh.

The body takes some water and washes her face.
She does indeed look for all the world like Rosa.
The dead man starts to stir too.

Beatriz

STOP. It's grotesque, stop!
What's happening?

Rosa pours some water for Tomas to wash in.
He washes the blood off his face. He drinks too.
He passes the water along to the next dead person, who
does the same. They wash the blood from their eyes.
Rosa smoothes down her dress, and gets a chair.

Rosa

It's so hot.
We should be sleeping. We should be flat on our backs
in the shade.

Beatriz

What?

Rosa

Pass me the cloth.

Beatriz

It's dirty, I just cleaned the table.

Rosa

The water then.

Beatriz

I'll wake up.
I'm thirsty, that's all, may brain . . .

Rosa

I used the lemon juice like you said.

She lifts her petticoat to look at her legs.

Don't think it did any good. Still black as anything.
Look.
Still, the worst kind of spider crawling up my legs.

Beatriz

Rosa?

Rosa

Of course, a little hair is beautiful. Women are supposed to have hair, but like mine? And my arms are the same. He thinks I'm beautiful, that is because the face and the neck and the head, I can work at, but the body – when the clothes are off . . . ?

Rosa brings a big table over.
She lays a cloth.

Beatriz

What are you doing?

Rosa

I'm getting ready for my wedding, isn't that what you said I should do?

Beatriz

I don't want to go back to the start.
Stop it!
Don't make me go back to the start.
It's day forty-one, for God's sake.

Rosa

Tonight he'll be so keen he'd go with any hairy animal, but tomorrow? And the day after?

Beatriz

Rosa?

Pause.

Rosa

Beatriz?
Are you OK?

She looks round at Beatriz for the first time.

Beatriz

I . . .

Rosa

And I've got veins.
I couldn't sleep for worrying about my veins.

Beat.

Beatriz

Is it really you?
I've been such a long way away.

Rosa

You say the strangest things.

Beatriz

I can smell the olives,
The goat.

Rosa

I wish you could make love with your clothes on.

Beatriz

You can.

Rosa

Some of them.
This has to be the hottest day of the year don't you think?

Beatriz

Am I really home?

Rosa

Madam Creole said she'd give us two chickens, did I tell you?
And Jan a wooden chair.

Beatriz

A wooden chair?

Rosa

Yes.
Well one is better than none.
I've done a little magic of my own.

What if I were to tell you there were three jugs of
wine behind the wheel?

Rosa goes to get the wine.

Beatriz

Can we slow down, Rosa,
Just talk for a bit?

Rosa

I'm getting married in a couple of hours.
What else is there to talk about?

Beatriz

I went outside of here. I saw the world, I saw some
terrible things.

Rosa comes back with the wine.

Rosa

Want a taste?

Beatriz

No.
It's you. It's you I want to touch.
Let me.
Rosa, please put your arms around me.

Rosa

I'm not married yet, anyway I'll only be across the
fields.

Beatriz

I never want to leave here again. I want to stay right
by your side. I love you, you know that, more than
anything.

Beatriz embraces her.
A man comes in, Pedro.

Pedro

I've been walking for twelve hours, I saw the house.
I thought you might have some water or something.

Beatriz

GO AWAY!

Pedro

The gate was open.

Beatriz

So go back out of it.

Pedro

What's in the jug?

Beatriz

Don't give him anything, if you give him anything
that brings the rest, and then the rest brings the girl.

A second man walks in, Juan.

Juan

Is that cake I can smell?

Beatriz

Oh God.

Rosa

Who are you talking to?

Juan

You've got oranges?

Rosa

Get off.

Rosa comes and grabs the second jug of wine.
The man grabs her.
She holds on to it.
The wine spills on the cloth.

You bloody idiot.

Pedro

You idiot.

Rosa
We could have drunk that.

Tomas come in.

Tomas
People are being killed, Rosa. Listen to me.

Beatriz
No.

Rosa
You brought them here?

Beatriz
Can't I stop them? If I see them off would it stop?

Tomas
They've been marching, they were thirsty.

Beatriz
Please no.

The Sergeant walks on.

Sargento
Are there beds here, can we sleep here?

Beatriz
It's like sand between my fingers.

Juan
The house looks well equipped, sir.

Tomas
I think we should leave them the house.

Beatriz
Tomas?

Sargento
Do an inventory.

Beatriz (*to Tomas*)
Take her away. Marry Rosa, then take her away.

Tomas

I think we should leave them the goat.

Beatriz

Why isn't he listening?

Sargento

You'll be paid for everything we use.

Rosa

In what?

Sargento

You write a chitty, I take it to the General.

Rosa

And he does what with it?
Wipes his arse?

Beatriz

I said that, not you.

Sargento

Clear this table, leave a chair.

Beatriz

Why did you say that, not me?

Rosa

This is all wit, surely. You are making me laugh. First
you are marching the wrong way, second there might
be food here but he has brought you into marsh land.

Beatriz

My words again.

Sargento

Tell me what to do, and you've saved your goat.

Beatriz

OK, let's get through the next bit, if this whole thing
is about the child, let's get to the child.
It's not a court, it's a soldiers' hearing,

You are the judge.
Bring on the child, but know this, I'll watch them kill her if that is what you want.
I'll stand back and do nothing as they tear her from limb to limb.
Is that what you want?
Huh, on the forty-first day? God?

The Girl is brought on.
She looks six again. Tiny. Innocent. Afraid.

Beatriz
    Shit.

Tomas
    Sir, she was crying a little way back.

Sargento
    So?

Tomas
    She was clawing at me to get through the gate.

Sargento
    You are bothering me about a child now.
    Is there any end to today?

Tomas
    She's Colline's daughter.
    The man you just sent away.
    But what shall I do with her?

Sargento
    Send her back to her mother.

Pedro
    Her mother is dead.

The Girl starts to whimper.

Beatriz
    Can someone not comfort her?

Sargento
What's it crying for?

Rosa
Its father probably.

Beatriz
I said that. Why do you keep saying what I said?

Juan
So we take it down the forest then?
Lose it.

Beatriz
Agreed.

Rosa
You're joking surely.

Beatriz
Rosa –

Rosa
Are you out of your mind?

Beatriz
Rosa, we've got to leave it.

Rosa
She –

Beatriz
She –

Rosa
She is six.

Beatriz
I know this sounds strange, and you'll find it hard to
believe, and I thought like you.

Rosa
Take it to its father.
He's only a minute ahead.

Beatriz

She isn't a regular child, she looks it but –

Pedro

The horses are all resting, sir.

Beatriz

It doesn't end well.

Sargento

There's a wheelbarrow by the well.

The men laugh.

Rosa

Why aren't you helping? I thought you of all people –

Beatriz

You don't know this child like I do.
It looks normal.

Rosa

She –

Beatriz

She –

Rosa

We'll find Daddy, eh?

Beatriz

Please, I'm begging you.

Rosa

I don't know what's happened to you.

Beatriz

The girl is evil, she'll suck you dry.

Rosa

Who are you, you look like my sister but –

Beatriz

She kills a thousand people, she poisons people's minds.

Rosa

When did you change?

Rosa takes the Girl's hand.

Beatriz

Sometimes in nature you get a bad one, a caterpillar turns yellow before it can make a pupa, a kid that dies before –

Rosa

You're not my sister.

Beatriz rushes at Rosa. She grabs her around the waist.

Beatriz

Of course I am.

Rosa struggles. She and Beatriz fight.
Rosa picks up a knife.

Rosa

I never thought I would fight you.

Beatriz rushes in again.
They struggle, Rosa's neck breaks.

Beatriz

Oh my God.

Rosa falls limp.

It was like butter, I hardly touched her.
Someone's neck can't break as easily as that.

The Girl stands.

Someone get some help!
My sister needs help –
HELP!

Sargento

What about the child?

Tomas
I'll take her.

Beatriz
What?

Tomas
Her father is just there.

Beatriz
Tomas, you can't take her.

Tomas
I'll be two minutes.

Beatriz
I can't kill you all.
Is this hell now, then? To relive one's mistakes a
thousand times?
Are you laughing now?

The Sergeant gives her the knife.

Sargento
You kill who you need to kill.
We have a war to fight.

Beatriz throws the knife down.

Beatriz
No, I can't do it.
You said you'd lose her, take her to the wood.
Oi.

The soldiers start to walk away just as they did before.

Sargento
It's late, we are all tired.

He walks out.

Beatriz
Don't leave me with this, you said you would do it.

Juan and Pedro walk past her.
Even Tomas walks out.

Tomas.

Tomas
I'm with the army now, I have to do as they tell me.

Beatriz
Don't just walk away. Oi, don't just walk away from me.
I'll curse you, I'll put a hex on all your houses.

They've gone.
Beatriz picks up the knife.

Every now and then, you get a bad one in nature,
a pupa that dies.

Beat.

I'll close my eyes, just run,
Go somewhere.
I'll count and I won't come after you.

The Girl doesn't move.

I'll make you run, I'll pinch you –
Run run run.
I can't do it again.
You and me, we didn't do well.
This is the end now, go.

A old man, Clement, comes in.
He's dressed as a simple farmer.
He gets the wheelbarrow from its place by the wall.

I've got a knife – don't touch me,
The soldiers are that way.

Clement
I won't touch you.

He lifts up the wheelbarrow.

The wheel is broken, but you can still use it.

Beatriz
Dad?

Clement
I'll put a nail across the axle, it will be fine.

Beatriz
You're back?

Clement
She's heavy, but you'll manage.

Beatriz
Dad, look at me.

Clement
And with a bit of wire around the handle –

Beatriz
Another mirage?
Dad, look at me.
I can't take her,
I got it all wrong.

Clement
No.

Beatriz
She ended up –

Clement
So try again.

Beatriz
Try again? Are you kidding. Am I in hell?

Clement
I don't know. Maybe.

Beatriz

I waited for you, every day for thirteen years.

Clement

And I've cleaned out the base, soldered the bottom.

Beatriz

Why didn't you come back?

Beat.

Clement

Don't ask me that.

Beatriz

I was four when you left.
I spent every day standing at the gate, looking for you.
I know your body was never found.

Clement

You'll need this as well.

He gives her the bag from Rossignol.

Beatriz

I can't do it.
Not again.
Every now and then you get a bad one in nature,
it would be better if she –

Clement

No.
She's six years old. Look at her.
Nothing is carved in stone.
Take the bag.
Beatriz, take the bag.

Beatriz

It's heavier.

Clement

I put in some extra things.

Beat.

Beatriz
  Will they make a difference?

The man shrugs.

Clement
  I hope so.

Beatriz puts the bag on her back.
She goes over to the Girl.
She gives her her hand.

Beatriz
  I don't even know her name.

Clement
  So ask her.

Beatriz
  What's your name?

Girl
  Oiseaux.

Beatriz
  Oiseaux?

The Girl takes her hand.

  OK, Oiseaux.
  OK.

Beatriz is back at the start. The journey is ahead.